Lya Luft was born in the state of Rio Grande do Sul in southern Brazil in 1938. She studied German and English and lectured as a professor of Linguistics in Porto Alegre for many years. With her first novel, *As Parceiras* [Partners], she captured the hearts of a wide readership and won over the critcs. She has since published 13 further works.

Today Lya is one of Brazil's most respected authors. When it was published in her native country *Losses and Gains* topped the bestseller list for months.

Losses and Gains

Gains

Reflections on a Life

Translated from the Portuguese
by Michael Wolfers

LYA LUFT

Vermilion
LONDON

1 3 5 7 9 10 8 6 4 2

Published in 2007 by Vermilion, an imprint of Ebury Publishing
First Published in Brazil by Récord in 2003

Ebury Publishing is a division of the Random House Group

The Random House Group Limited Reg. No. 954009

Addresses for companies within the Random House Group can be found at
www.randomhouse.co.uk

A CIP catalogue record for this book is available from the British Library

The Random House Group Limited makes every effort to ensure that the
papers used in our books are made from trees that have been legally
sourced from well-managed and credibly certified forests. Our
paper procurement policy can be found on
www.randomhouse.co.uk

Typeset by SX Composing DTP, Rayleigh, Essex
Printed in the UK by CPI Cox & Wyman, Reading, RG1 8EX

ISBN 9780091912970

For Fabiana and Fernanda – and Rodrigo – who form part of the gains

From the age of six I had a mania for drawing the forms of things. By the time I was 50, I had published an infinity of designs; but all that I have produced before the age of 70 is not worth taking into account. At 73 I have learned a little about the real structure of nature, of animals, plants, trees, birds, fish and insects. In consequence, when I am 80, I shall have made more progress; at 90 I shall penetrate the mystery of things; at 100 I shall certainly have reached a marvellous stage, and when I am 110, everything I do, be it a dot or a line, will be alive.

(Hokusai Katsushika, 1760–1849)

Contents

Foreword

I WAS VERY happy to learn that the English-speaking public
should have this opportunity to read one of the most influential
Brazilian women writers of today. Lya Luft is one of those rare
authors with the gift of opening up pathways.

I say pathways and not short-cuts, since her work addresses
not a simplification but the richness of life. In times of easy fixes
and the cult of the new and the young, Lya invites us to do
things that are increasingly rare today: to mature and to see the
beauty of each stage of life, and to face with optimism the
passage of time.

Lya Luft trained in Anglo-German letters and took her
master's in Brazilian literature. She lectured and she built a solid
career as a translator from German and from English, turning
into Portuguese works of such authors as Thomas Mann,
Günter Grass, Virginia Woolf and many others. In 1980, when
she was 41, she embarked on a career of fiction with the
publication of the novel *As Parceiras* [Partners] – and she has
not ceased to amaze with sensitive and rich texts that win over
critics and readers. But it was with *Perdas e Ganhos* [Losses and
Gains], in 2003, that Lya reached the general public.

Losses and Gains

With a light touch, this book speaks of themes of concern to the lives of us all and bears witness to the author's unique capacity to win over readers with whom she makes friends: touching the soul and making them think; welcoming and inspiring. Life for Lya must be lived with passion and savoured for its sweet and bitter gifts. It is scarcely surprising that, after her established success as novelist, poet and translator, she has revealed an unparalleled sensitivity in her texts in the genre of moral instruction.

Losses and Gains brings to the reader the reflections of a mature woman on fundamental themes, such as the passage of time, maturity, ageing, family relationships, death, isolation, love, self-esteem, motherhood. From the minutiae to the monumental in life, she enhances the most significant aspects of our existence, with the delicacy of someone looking at the world with optimism, but likewise with the strength and bluntness of someone who makes no concessions to trivia.

Lya Luft is an optimist, but she does not see the human being through rose-tinted glasses. Her reflections are often disturbing; they provoke and invite the contemporary man and woman to be in touch with themselves, to look within, and to grow.

Which of us, young or mature, has not experienced life's joys and disappointments, victories and defeats, losses and gains? One of the author's great teachings is that the outcome of these equations in life offers is ultimately dependent on what we can understand. She demonstrates that making the most of life and of humanity, accepting the passage of time and maturing will help us escape traps we set ourselves – that block the vision of the transcendent and essential.

Foreword

Lya does not teach formulas or present lessons. In *Losses and Gains* she shares with the reader personal testimony on the experience of maturing. She thereby helps to open up pathways, demonstrating the countless possibilities that life brings at all its stages, from youth to the age of maturity. In this fascinating and revealing work, readers will constantly find a little of themselves, of their experiences, fears, doubts and anxieties. They will find the resonance we crave so much in relationships with others.

Paulo Coelho

I

Invitation

I AM NOT the sand
where a pair of wings is sketched
or bars before a window.
I am not merely a rolling stone
on the world's tides,
on every beach rebirthing another.
I am an ear clamped to the shell
of life, I am construction and demolition,
servant and master, and I am
mystery.

Hand in hand let us write the script
for the theatre of my time:
my destiny and I.
We are not always in tune,
nor do we always take ourselves
seriously.

Finding the tone

What is this book?

Perhaps a complement to my 1996 essay *Rio do Meio*. I write along the same lines, taking up some of my usual themes. All my work is elliptical or circular: plots and characters peek here and there behind a new mask. I do this because I have not exhausted their potential, and I go on telling them. I shall probably carry on in this way to the last line of the final book.

So what is this book?

I shall not call it 'essays', because the solemn tone and the theoretical underpinning suggested by the term are not my style. Certainly not novel or fiction. Nor is it a teaching – I do not have this to give.

As in many fields of activity, new methods of work and creativity arise that need new names. Everyone will give this narrative the name they wish. For me it is that same word in the listener's ear, which I find so pleasing and use in novels or poems – a call for the reader to come and think with me.

What I write is born out of my own maturing, a path of highs and lows, shining moments and shadowy areas. On this route, I learned that life does not weave a web only of losses but furnishes us with a succession of gains.

The balance of the scales depends largely on what we can and want to perceive.

$\sim$

I meet a friend, a distinguished pianist, and I report that I am beginning a book, but, as always at the start of a new work, I am still looking for the right 'tone'.

Invitation

He finds that apt, a writer looking for the tone. We laugh, because we find in the end that both of us are looking for the same thing: our tone. The tone of our language, of our art, and – this is true of anybody – the tone of our life. In what tone do we wish to live it? (I did not ask how we are *condemned* to live.)

In melancholy semi-tones, in brighter tones, with speed and superficiality, or alternating joy and pleasure with profound and thoughtful moments?

Only skimming the surface or from time to time diving into deep waters?

Distracted by the noise around or listening to the voices in the pauses and the silence – our own voice, the other's voice?

Will our tone be one of suspicion and mistrust or will it open portals to an endless landscape?

It depends partly on us.

In the instrument of our orchestration, we are – along with genetic or random accidents – the tuners and the performers. Prior to this, we construct our instrument. This makes the assignment more difficult, but much more stimulating.

I sit here at the computer and I think about the tone of this book, which I must find. At this starting point I sense it as a whisper to the reader: 'Come and think with me, come and help me in the quest.'

Although it is a private word, this might at some moments seem a cruel book: I say that we are important, and good, and capable, but I say too that we are often futile, we are too often mediocre. I say that we could be very much happier than we usually allow ourselves to be, but we are afraid of the price to be paid. We are cowards.

Nevertheless, the book must be hopeful: I am one of those who believe that happiness is possible, love is possible, that there is not merely missed opportunity and betrayal but tenderness, friendship, compassion, ethics and delicacy.

I think that on the route of our existence we need to learn this discredited practice known as 'being happy'. (I see eyebrows raised ironically before this romantic declaration of mine.)

Each one on his path and with his particular characteristics.

∼

In art as in human relations, including a variety of loving relationships, we swim against the current. We attempt the impossible: total fusion does not exist, complete sharing is impossible to achieve. The essence cannot be shared: it is discovery and surprise, the glory or damnation of each – in isolation.

However, in a conversation or a silence, in a gaze, in a loving gesture as in a work of art, a narrow window may open up. Together, the performer and his spectator or his reader will stare – like two lovers.

That is how people, skinning knees and hands, end up.

So I write and shall write: to stimulate my imaginary reader – substitute for the imaginary friends of childhood? – to search within and to share with me so many anxieties about what we are doing with the time that is allotted to us.

Since living must be – until the last thought and the final gaze – a process of self-transformation.

What I write here is not mere daydreams. I am a woman of my time, and I want to bear witness to it with all the skill I can:

giving scope to my fantasies or writing about pain and puzzlement, contradiction and grandeur; about disease and death. Regretting the word spoken at the wrong time and the silence when it would have been better to speak out.

I write continually about the way we are simultaneously to blame and innocent in regard to what happens to us.

We are authors of a good part of our choices and omissions, daring or compromise, our hope and comradeship or our mistrust. Above all, we must decide how we employ and enjoy our time, which is in the end always our present time.

But we are innocent of accidents and brute chance that rob us of perfect loves, people, health, employment and security.

As a result my perspective of the human being, of my self, is as contrary as we provocatively are.

We are transition, we are process. This disturbs us.

The flow of days and years, decades, serves growth and increment, not loss and restriction. In this perspective, we become masters, not servants; human beings, not frightened little animals that scurry away without knowing exactly why.

If my reader and I can agree on our reciprocal tone, this initial monologue will be a dialogue – even though I may never gaze upon the countenance of the other who in the end becomes a part of me.

So my art shall have achieved some kind of goal.

2

Drawing in the depth of the mirror

FRUIT OF MISTAKES or of love,
I am born from my own contradiction.
The twist of the mouth,
the shape of the hand, the trick of walking
(dreams and fears included)
will come from those who have shaped me.
But what I would trace in the mirror
has to be armed as well
according to my desire.

I shall have my pair of wings
whose flight rises from those
who give me the shade where I grow
– just as, under a tree,
a stalk
and its flower.

The brand on the flank

The world has no subsistence without our perception that imbues it with form, without our thinking that gives it order.

It is an astonishing idea: we live according to our point of view, with which we survive or are shipwrecked. We explode or coagulate according to whether we are open or closed to the world.

And what shapes this perspective of ours?

It begins in childhood, with deficiencies not always explicable. Even if we were loved, we may suffer a basic insecurity. Although protected, we may be exposed to accidents and eventualities against which we have no defence. We have to create barricades and simultaneously make bridges to our surroundings and what is in store. All this plot of meeting and separation, conjoined terror and ecstasy, the material of our existence, begins before we are born.

But we are not merely swept on a torrent by default. *We are participants.*

Here lies our potential tragedy: the squandering of a life with its talents cut short if we do not succeed in seeing or if we lack the audacity to change to improve – at any moment, and at any age.

The foundation of this 'we' begins in childhood, raises its walls in maturity and culminates in the rooftop in old age, which is a crowning achievement although generally taken as a deterioration.

In this work our hand joins with the hands of the many who shape us. By breaking free of them with maturity, we shall demonstrate our stature: the person we wish to be, who we think we should be – who we think we *deserve to be*.

In this house, the house of the soul and the house of the body, we shall not be mere aimless puppets but warriors who think and decide.

To constitute a human being, the 'we' is a job that has no days off and allows no rest: there will be fragile walls, faulty calculations, cracks. Perhaps a section will collapse. But the job will also open windows on the landscape and portals to the sun.

What is produced – a habitable house or a sterile ruin – will be the sum of what was thought of us and we think of ourselves, the extent to which we were loved and we love, what others made us think we were worth and what we did to confirm or change this, this seal, signet, or brand.

However this is still too simple: in this mortar are mixed good faith and evasion, seduction and celebration, loving words and invitations refused. We participate in an extraordinary dance of donned masks, behind which we are the object of our own disquiet. Not totally victims or totally masters, with every moment of every day a challenge.

This ambiguity wounds us and nurtures us. It makes us human.

Within the timetable of my existence I shall fulfil the project that was offered to me, gradually taking charge of the canvas and the brush.

In the early years almost everything was the work of the environment in which I was born: family, school, windows through which they taught me to observe – shelter or cage, expectation or condemnation.

Soon I shall no longer have the others as excuse: father and mother, loving or hostile, warm-hearted or indifferent, suffering all the natural ills of the human condition that only as adults we recognise. In the end we must note: my father, my mother, were only people as I am. They did what they knew, what they could.

And me . . . and me?

Marked by what we transmit to others, we shall be acrobats in our own circus. The net stretched below is woven from two intertwined wires: one is born from those who begot and reared us; the other comes from us, from our belief or our hope.

~

I often heard in my childhood: 'A child doesn't think.'

A child does think. And does something else more important, something that we unlearn as we mature: the child *is*. In contemplating a stain on the wall, an insect in the grass or the miracle of a rose, the child is not only gazing. The child *is being* everything on which he is concentrating. *He is* the beetle, the figure on the wall, *he is* flower, wind and silence.

In the same way *he is* the coldness or the anguish of adults, superficiality or their genuine love.

Sometimes he must be left in peace, without demanding that he be always on the go, running, talking, playing, as if contemplation were a disease.

The child immersed in his surroundings is taking a part in a process greater than himself, in which he blossoms unconsciously. But he has something more precious than consciousness: intuition about everything, an *innocent wisdom*.

We shall lose this innocent wisdom to the extent to which we are tamed, necessarily locked into the surrounding reality.

God willing, people in this process of being tamed can retain the capacity to dream, since utopia will be the terrain of our freedom. Or we shall end up like trained seals carrying out our tasks meticulously, but burying what we call psyche, ego, self, or simply *soul*.

We shall be gnawed by futility, as deadly as the worst disease: it attacks the soul, leaving it porous and fractured like some skeletons.

A soul with osteoporosis.

A child is above all his own dimension in which time, odours and textures, presences and emotions are his idiosyncratic reality.

As a child I sometimes tried to explain this in my faltering words. Nobody seemed to understand – or they were not very interested. So I put it all into stories I would tell myself like witches' incantations. As an adult I ended up doing much the same by writing novels and other books – such as this.

I understood that the apparent indifference of others to my childish imaginings was not because they were uninterested or because I was not able to give a clear explanation. It was because the imagination and the real cannot be distinguished or contained in words, and thus cannot be communicated.

~

Once again a book of mine is based on the idea of the family.

I have written tirelessly about it.

We are marked by the prophetic gaze cast upon us when we are small, like the curse or blessing of the fairies in children's stories.

Losses and Gains

The dramatic or tragic characters I invented in my novels were the crop of particularly sick families where lovelessness, hypocrisy and isolation ruled. Sometimes they were inhibited by the impossibility of showing affection – the latter withered without expression.

If living alone is hard enough, living in a family can be fraught and burdensome. We suffer from the precariousness of loving bonds. We suffer from a shortage of money and time. We suffer from the growing necessity to overcome the demands of consumerism. We suffer from the limited scope for dialogue, tenderness, solidarity within the home. Principally, we have no time or disposition for the natural expression of the joy of affection.

Children in any family will certainly not be primarily a problem and a duty. If they are to bring us joy we must want and love them. Making the home a nest, not a cage, will begin before that first touch and gaze upon a newborn child.

Childhood is the ground on which we shall traverse the rest of our days. If it has too many pitfalls we shall be more prone to stumble, fall more easily and smash our face – which might even be healthy, since it would give us the opportunity to rebuild our countenance. Perhaps a more genuine countenance. But sometimes we shall be left paralysed.

In full maturity I sense within me the small girl astounded by the beauty of the rain that falls on the trees in a garden of many decades ago. All of that is in me for ever, even if the beloved people go away, the house is sold, and I am no longer that girl.

I therefore needed to make room in myself for a space where I could shelter the positive elements, and I wanted it to be greater than the site where inevitably I should store the relics.

The outline of this *me* must be broadened by my skill, so that, within all my limitations, I can open myself and welcome a life in continual transformation.

Much of the time we go about half blind, advancing through trial and error, tiptoeing through the challenges of every day. On such firm soil or treacherous sand we must construct our personal house *in part* from these raw materials. Not everything can be programmed. The calculations have unexpected results. Mingled within us are the possibility of dreaming and the necessity of crawling – fear and fervour.

It may be utopian, but I shall not allow my sensitivity to be deadened as I grow old. Instead of being parched I shall have reached the utmost expression of my affections.

~

Everything is complicated because we carry our psychic baggage. *We are born from the evolution that we are*: something in us is immutable; our essence makes walls difficult to scale, too strong to allow breaches. This battle will go on for our entire existence.

The tools for us to fulfil the task of living may be precarious. This means some people are born more fragile than others. A baby may be more sorrowful than his livelier sibling. It is not a judgement, but a warning from Mother Nature.

My tiny garden teaches me daily that there are plants that are born strong, others misshapen; some are attacked by blight or death in youthful prime, others in twisted old age continue to flower.

We share the same condition, with a startling difference: we can think. We can enjoy relative freedom. Within certain limits, we can intervene.

So once again *we are responsible*, for ourselves. We are at the very least *jointly responsible* for what we do with the baggage we were given for this journey between birth and death.

We carry much useless weight. On the way we abandon things that might be precious and we collect irrelevancies. We run without stopping until that dreaded end; we rarely stop and stare, judge the road, and change or maintain our personal project.

Or we do not even have personal desires. We adulterate ourselves in the waters of fate or other people's will. We remain too feeble to react. We are the ones crouching in the corners or sitting on the edge of the sofa in the salons of life.

Every waste of a destiny, an individual who denies himself natural development according to his capability or beyond, seems to me as tragic and significant as war, since it is the defeat of one human being – worth as much as thousands.

We should not write articles and join marches only against war, violence, corruption and poverty, but should proclaim the significance of what has been sown in us as individuals, and how we should husband the time that was given to us for this remarkable gardening.

~

If I insist on the significance of the fundamental gaze leading me by one path or another, might I not be putting too much primary blame on the family – on the parents?

I think this is so.

The primary love, that between parents and children, will determine our expectation of all the loves we shall have. Our initial experience will impact on many of our future experiences.

So child-bearing and rearing means begetting and giving birth to them again every day, without respite.

All love entails or is a crisis; all love demands patience, good humour, tolerance and strength in dosages that are always uncertain. There are no prescriptions or training schools to teach how to love. An arena of destructive battles prevents me from being a whole person – as does the artificial comfort of problems overlooked. Struggles can be positive, competition leads to growth; loving means imposing and accepting boundaries.

The family relationship occurs between differing or even antagonistic personalities, predestined to live a long while between the four walls of the same house (without the possibility of divorce if they are parents and children), coupled in a bubbling cauldron of missed opportunities and disagreements: 'I always felt that my mother did not really know what to do with me!'

'My child even as a baby always seemed uncomfortable in my arms.'

'I never understood what my father really wanted from me, he was always a stranger.'

'Something chemical, in the skin, did not work between my mother and me, we did not like to hug.'

'We always lived in different worlds, remote from one another.'

'I was never able to please my mother, she criticised me all the time, and even now that I am adult and she is elderly, we continue in the same tone.'

'My father seemed vexed just seeing me. He demanded everything of me. However hard I tried, I always felt I owed him something.'

This family group that we do not choose and that defines us so much could be a safe port from which we embark and to which we can return, even in our thoughts. That place will always be *my place*, even though I no longer live there.

But it is essential to break with what will eventually stifle, since it could also be a cage, an abyss, the pit of a well. If we remain too trapped, we shall have to tug ourselves by our own hair to another space where even with fear and uncertainty we can breathe and decide what to do next.

We cannot change the past. Family dramas may have poisonous roots beneath the soil of our relationships or our soul. The law of silence, of obsessive secrecy, may constitute serious disturbance. But we can change our attitude in regard to all this, albeit through long and sorrowful processes that will mean the difference between life and death.

I can free myself. I can reprogramme myself to discern what is for me, at this moment, the 'best' action – or its potential.

My concept of the world inhibits my decisions and devours me and makes me back off, or compels me to face up to alternatives. At this juncture my innate baggage comes into play: what I have built in myself, the resources on which I can call – and my confidence in my ability to do something.

We do not control the destiny of the people we love, still less can we suffer in their place, but having children means taking on a serious responsibility. Not only for food, schooling, health, but for the personality of these children: more complex a task than ensuring healthy physical survival.

This does not mean that we shape or distort them like omnipotent gods. On the contrary, it is part of the drama of fathering and mothering and we cannot live for them or shield them from their fates or make their choices. But certainly our way of being, living and thinking when they were little, when they still seemed to be 'ours', will have a bearing on all this.

I am not defending victim parents, who 'out of love for their children' surrender their own lives. I do not admire the sacrificial mother who denies her own personality with the same excuse, and at heart blames the children and charges them for what they 'owe' her and even what they 'do not owe'.

But it will be based on us, our hope or despair, our affection or coldness, that the children will take the first of their many steps. As they will do in turn with their children in the future. This will be as fundamental for them as our parents' parents were in the previous generation.

Before and behind every human couple stretches a long chain of failures and successes as generators of humanity.

~

We are born with all the baggage of our genetic make-up both physical and psychic. *But we are not that alone.* We are in part the outcome of what our parents were. *But we are not that alone.*

The society in which we live has many eyes and arms, which watch over us and intervene in our reality. One of those is called *outside opinion*. Not that of people we love and respect, but that amorphous entity, omnipresent and almost omnipotent, of 'what will they think?'. Without asking permission it comes into our house and our consciousness, disabling and pruning back.

Outside the walls of the home, our cultural integration has unheard-of strength. To overcome it we need discernment, not youth's characteristic talent. Until we reach maturity we are much more vulnerable to this external pressure that over-whelms us and takes command.

As an adolescent in an interior citadel where behaviour was dictated by this faceless creature – or one of many faces – I had strong backing in what was taught in my house: outside opinion was really of no interest. There would be a few people to whom out of respect and affection I would want to render account – they would be my references in many matters.

Much of what they bequeathed us can be reprogrammed: we are a product but not slaves, the primordial gaze that hailed us is not necessarily a death sentence. We can – thankless task – make our additions, write an 'erratum' on the text of this prefatory 'us'.

But who will give us suggestions, who can help us – if we are also preformed, prefabricated and conditioned? Who is going to unweave these wires – these wires where we begin and the influence of so many others ends?

We are therefore seekers, restless, naturally unsatisfied. *We are not condemned*: we are free for many decisions. From the age when I attained some level of discernment, what did I do to continue being – or improving – what I am now? How was I becoming an individual who cultivates freedom but also respect and tenderness for the other? How did I situate myself in relation to that anonymous and powerful entity that is called *other people*, which can be lovable yet cruel?

Our vague vision has more definition with maturity and reflection. What we call personality takes shape – our own opinion, attitude. In a thousand ways we reveal the place we propose to occupy: through our choice of clothes, profession, partner, everything. Above all in the unconscious I shall behave according to the confidence, doubt, enthusiasm or scepticism that characterise me.

When I gave faculty classes I would insist with the young: 'You are better than you think. You are more intelligent and more talented than you think, than, what we adults – parents and teachers – unwittingly make you believe you are.'

We teach our children that they are beautiful and good, that they are princes of the spirit; or do we make them feel wretched, nuisances, objects of worry and distaste, rows and regret, launched on an adventure doomed to failure?

Why do we create submissive souls when we could make free souls?

The question might seem cynical in the light of the complexity of our social structures and opportunities for development, but it merits explanation. In suggesting that our children must feel like princes and princesses, it is obvious that I am not thinking of luxury and social status, much less arrogance, attribute of the mediocre.

Self-esteem is what I have in mind.

A positive vision, not rose-tinted or unreal, signifying confidence. With a capacity for joy, the quest for happiness, beliefs. What more can I do, as a whole and happy being, within my potential – that generally builds on what we believe or what it makes us believe. Therefore I would tell my students: you are better than you think.

Self-esteem reminds me of what my beloved friend the writer Erico Verissimo used to say: 'I love myself, I do not admire myself.'

It has to do with overcoming the comfortable spirit of the herd: to shape and maintain one's own views. Not by living disdainfully on the margin, but by facing up to the risk of some isolation. Not by selling the soul at any price for some company, but by choosing the selected loved ones, loyal friends, sensible tutors and models. Not even by picking the most appropriate profession, the one that gives us most pleasure if we can make this choice: we have to grasp any activity when it is a matter of survival.

Easy to say . . . I know.

Change brings anxiety.

Trying to leave a job where I am badly paid or I am unhappy; facing an oppressive father or mother; breaking a loving relationship that shrinks or crushes me; avoiding an encounter where one allows someone else to ride roughshod over me in a process of servitude that generates resentment and guilt.

Leaving the established and the customary, even if ruinous, is always unsettling.

The desire to be more free and strong, the fear of leaving a known situation, however bad it may be, can be even worse. For us to reorganise ourselves, we must uncouple, remake this enigma of ours and discover what in the end is the project for each of us.

~

'But the family no longer has the significance you attribute it,' you will object. 'People are much freer, obligations less restrictive. Everything has changed.'

No: *nearly everything* has changed. The essence remains the same: the essential us.

Society has seen hectic change over the past century: the family changed, the culture transformed, science and technology evolved; everything moves on at a speed unimaginable 50 years ago.

However, human emotions have not changed.

Still less are we originals. Our basic desires must be the same: security, affection, freedom, companionship; to feel that I am integrated in society or in the family, to be important to my peers or at least to one person – the one who is my love. I do not need to be a king to be important, but I must feel that *I am valued*.

This has defined me as much as the first gaze that fell upon me. I must regard myself as capable and worthy, without megalomania, without alienation, within what is available for me to choose, adapt, make my own.

It has nothing to do with money, social status or pride, but with the way we are assessed – by ourselves and by those whom we love. My acts and withdrawals are born from this primary concept.

It matters not if I am workman, maid, driver, peasant or senior manager, award-winning actress or humble shop assistant: I like myself insofar as I have faith in my dignity, and I want to grow in accordance with my worth. It is also according to the value I place on this leap, this growth, this delivery. It depends on my confidence.

All this was not instilled in us through words rehearsed for special occasions or crises. It is structured subliminally in daily encounters, it lurks in the environment, shines in the role.

I return to the family: a tough environment at home will not prepare someone to face the toughness of life, as some argue. On the contrary: to be able to defend myself on the violent terrain where we live I need a firm grounding in affection.

This is the most important nourishment I can be given from the cradle. It nurtures my soul, and it enables me to secure my place: my place in my home, in my marriage, in my family, in my classroom, in my office, in my factory, in my street. But it must above all be my place within myself. It should not be subordinate.

If I believe that I am worth nothing, I shall be nothing. I shall leave others to speak, decide and live for me. However, if I believe that despite the natural limits and all the fears I deserve a share of positive things, I shall struggle for that.

I shall go so far as to allow others to love me.

~

Gestures, silences, words: living creatures that in the shadow of the unconscious arm attachments and disarm lives.

With them we build bridges over muddy waters or hew out the ditch of misunderstandings. A substantial amount of suffering between people is born from missed opportunity and lack of communication.

'I was always sure that our parents preferred you.'

'But how! I was always quite sure that they liked you much more.'

'You never told me that you loved me. I even believed that I was not your child, that I was adopted!'

'But how! I took care of you, sheltered you, taught you, gave you everything in my power. I wore myself out working more than I should so that you should not go short of anything. I washed your clothes, nursed you when you were ill . . .'

'But there was the time you said . . . you did . . . you seemed . . .'

'But it was nothing like that! You didn't understand properly. I was not able to explain myself fully.'

If the wound is too severe, dialogue and explanations such as these will not cure what has been engrained. It is not enough to have a Christmas night or a family lunch to undo the harm.

Someone told me: 'That's how it is, people don't understand one another. We are all poor devils, all complex, all insecure and unhappy: how can we hand on something good to our children?'

I do not agree.

I do not believe we are poor devils, or that we are all unhappy.

We are complex, that is true: plotters, vulnerable and subject to mistake and error. We are also amazing machines of affection and ideas, of dreams, of creation of art that takes us beyond the trivial. Capable of establishing the simplest routine that gives security and comfort.

However love – like lovelessness – is a demanding task, one that produces us and recreates us every hour. A personality is a game of loving with threaded feelings, with pieces difficult to arrange.

~

'They always told me that I was ugly,' someone recounted to me, 'and I convinced myself that I did not deserve to be valued, to be chosen – in short, to be happy.'

Someone else said to me: 'I was chubby, but my father would always stress that I had beautiful eyes, was intelligent, was loved. Without saying it specifically, he taught me that I should take care of my physical side, but the physical was not the be-all and end-all, and should not decide my destiny. Today, if someone should fail to love me because I do not fit the patterns set by fashion, that person would not persuade me to his way of thinking.'

~

The family provides us with the first criteria we can follow or break. Transgressing them may be salvation in many cases, for if they overwhelm us, escaping is not just a difficult but a heroic task. Either we free ourselves as much as possible, or they will be lurking behind the door at any moment, hands on hips, showing their face and pronouncing their sentence. That will be neither freedom nor absolution.

I was taught early on that my freedom was essential, that it was linked to my dignity, and that I would be responsible for my choices. Moreover, I knew that even if everything went wrong someone would always be there for me.

This became for me the basic concept of the family: *that group or person who, even if it or he did not understand me and sometimes did not approve, would respect me and love me as I am – or how I manage to be.*

At any stage this basic feeling of approval would be missed: yes, I deserve a good life. Later, positive experiences, personal effort and sentimental re-education could enhance and raise the level of our self-esteem.

Self-knowledge, one of the aims of therapy, clarifies the vision and leads to better understanding, to bearing wounds and to keeping one's head above water even when the wave is strong and ugly. To feel oneself valued by someone, be they friend or lover, or a group, can be definitive.

But not everything works out like that.

Something elementary might have been more damaging than we could bear. Fatally wounded at the outset, we shall spend our time peering in every direction: who is going to hurt me now, where is the next blow coming from, the next betrayal? In growing, maturing and ageing, what gaze do we turn upon ourselves?

Do we eventually stop to stand and stare?

Our way of seeing and living reflects – and replicates – the way we were seen when we were only a reflection in the mirror. Or shall we shape our own posture with all the effort and pain this may demand?

In our contradictions, we blend hesitation and fear with courage and fervour. We can hide in the dark room or turn our face towards the sun, alternate the two attitudes, squander and consume, hoard and multiply. We are all this. Our own amnesty or our own annihilation.

It is not only the fault of others if we remain curtailed. At every stage we can make a mark, a point, a colour in the project of what we seek to be.

We may be compelled to don disguises, but at our very heart resounds the name we give ourselves, our stamp of identity.

Theories of the soul

The more resources we have in the field of psychology and in new findings on human relations, the more insecure we are.

The more civilised we are, the less natural we are. This in an era when the more talk there is of nature the further we are from it. Being natural has come to be unnatural.

That is the way with bringing up offspring. Perplexed in the face of a thousand theories knocking on our door in all the media, and the proliferation of consulting rooms with every kind of therapy (for the most bizarre reasons), we are persuaded that to have and bring up a child is not very natural.

We are going from the old extreme of thinking that *a child does not think* to another extreme: *a child is a complication*. A thousand recipes for treatment from babyhood to adolescence torment generations of troubled parents. Trouble is not a good counsellor. In haste we even make love quite badly . . .

We forget the best teacher: common sense. Listening to what we have within, that old thing called intuition, do you remember? Obviously for this to work we must *have* common sense and have *something* within us to be heard.

Or every time the baby cries bitterly, the child is less active (often when he is merely thinking, wants after all to be left in peace for a while), we rush off to find a specialist. For him to teach us to hold the baby, breastfeed, look in the eye, snuggle to the bosom our child.

It is because we are troubled and disoriented. We have lost the habit of observing and reflecting. We prefer to avoid the mirror that makes us look within ourselves. We are maturing increasingly late or badly. We are children having children.

We do not like to reflect and decide. 'If I stop to think about my life, I shall collapse!' someone told me. We are afraid of finding the end of the wire hidden in the confusion of novelty, and by pulling on it see everything fall apart.

But this might be positive: we could gather up the pieces and start again. Perhaps create a more natural and viable interior than the one with which we began and on that give the children a calm and positive legacy – and message – not to be found in books and consulting rooms.

Being natural is in serious crisis.

~

When the sophistication of practices and tools becomes almost routine, we tend to employ complex strategies as well when it would be enough to rely on simplicity and sense. Even in environments where close affections predominate, there begins before birth a confusion generated by some vague theories or daft recipes that have nothing to do with the science of psychology, but with what I call *magazine psychologism*.

I want to reaffirm my appreciation of practitioners in the so-called psi field. Four years of therapy helped me through an extremely difficult period. Whenever I can I pay homage to the outstanding practitioner who guided me.

More than in most professions, this is a territory that we attain because we are suffering. We are vulnerable, and we do not know the byways of this new place. Forsaken, we are handed over to the practitioner who is going to take care of us.

I have observed some young women who attend their patients, adult or adolescent, in clothes more suited to a nightclub than to the gravity of a consulting room. I never tire of commenting that in the surgery we shall do something even more serious than patching the innards on an operating table: we shall try to patch our poor soul.

The appearance of young girls – miniskirts, sundresses, heavy make-up, using childish gestures when speaking – can disguise a highly commendable baggage of information and theories. But I, who am neither prurient nor judgemental, wonder if they inspire confidence in the afflicted who seek them out, if they can offer patients support and, above all, guidance.

I am reminded here of the story of a group of house doctors making a round with their professor through a hospital ward. One of the young women doctors, scantily dressed, sought out the teacher and whispered, 'Professor, when I came close, the patient in bed 14 began to masturbate.'

The professor looked her up and down, and said calmly, 'My girl, cover yourself up.'

I do not think that practitioners in the psi field should be venerable matrons. But they should not cause further disturbance to those who turn to them by showing them their own soul in a miniskirt.

It might seem quirky, but I take this very seriously.

I take being serious very seriously.

I take seriously the seriousness of disease, whether of the body or the mind, the need for shelter and succour that leads people to seek doctors of the body and heart.

And all this applies to the figures of father and mother within the home.

The father should not be an executioner or a brother: he has to be father, shoulder and hug; authority, lodestone and shelter; comradeship but firmness too.

A mother should not be a little friend, she should be *mother*. She should be someone to whom her children, even as adults, know they can turn when everything has failed them, even their best friends. She should not be the bogus bright young thing competing in make-up and clothes with her daughter, or appearing seductive to her son's colleagues, thereby creating constraints that she ignores as if she did not live in the real world.

Rather unattractive, unforgiving concepts?

Life can be much more unforgiving than that.

~

Loving is giving a child the means of acquiring a balanced personality.

You may ask what this balance is, and I shall answer that everyone has his own. It must be sufficient to prevent our drowning at the first wave. This requires neither extensive training nor great material wealth. It is not done though theory or debate, but through providing a welcoming lap, a firm hand and an attentive ear.

The potholes in the ground of our past were not that we were given only two pairs of trainers and trousers, none of the modern electronic toys, no ballet or language classes. The flaws in the terrain where we shall fall and break both heart and face are provoked by a hostile environment, by ill-prepared or unhappy parents. They are more harmful than poverty, plain clothing, a simple house, a suburban neighbourhood, a sink school or overwork. Solid ground will come from loving relationships, good humour, kindness and concern.

But how can we have this if routine is abandoned and we do not even communicate properly within the home? Loving is a luxury if we often lack time to read the newspaper, money to last out the month, joy to begin the day.

Hence I say that *begetting and giving birth is a serious responsibility*. We shall go on giving birth – to more than bodies – to complex human beings.

The fragility of family relationships or the eventual catastrophes, our insecurities, and the deluge of contradictory messages we can scarcely understand are making education increasingly difficult. So we delegate this to the crèche, the kindergarten, the school, the psychologist, classmates.

As we have little time, nobody can reasonably demand that on top of everything else we should show our feelings and talk when we arrive home exhausted from trying to sustain the family with the consumer demands it makes – or we think we are obliged to supply.

Even if begetting and giving birth physically is natural, *rearing is integrating oneself into a culture that overrides the natural*. It may be repetitive and tedious, problematic. We are going from the extreme of strict education to simplistic uneducation.

~

I knew education when it used to bring terror even in structured and functional families (before the findings of psychology would teach us to be less cruel).

'If you swallow the seeds, a tree will be born in your belly tonight; if you tell a lie, your nose will grow and a policeman will come to cut it off with enormous scissors; if you eat fruit without washing it, you will have a belly full of horrible worms . . .'

Today we have gone to the other extreme.

Parents, baffled by the invasion of a glib and not always coherent psychologism, are afraid to impose boundaries on their children to avoid them being 'traumatised'. Insecure or ill-informed parents take their children to the most diverse specialists for treatments that are not always necessary and appropriate. I know of parents who go to a hospital accident department for the nurses to cut their baby's nails, or to take a temperature merely because 'Today I think he is a little overheated.' Or because 'The baby cried without stopping three hours ago, he must have a pain somewhere' . . . and the doctor observes that he needs only a bath and clean nappies.

Cutting nails and popping in a thermometer are not an emergency. Dirty nappies are not an emergency.

A lack of love and attention could be an emergency.

Psychology helps an understanding and release of the personality but does not shape it. Likewise school, crèche, kindergarten are not the home or the family, teachers are not mothers or aunts. However worthy and respectable these third parties are, we should not unload on them the duties of our own heart.

What are these duties?

To free a space for tenderness in the hurried and difficult, potentially ruthless, day-to-day routine. To leave open the gate to meaningful dialogue, at a set time, but within the habitual flow of concern and warmth. Love in the family is an art, a juggling, sometimes a deed of heroism. Essential, like the air we breathe.

Preparing someone to live is not done with phrases, but by living together, preparing him for future relations, in order one day to have a job, a family, a life, and to make him human, tender, generous, strong and ethical.

Becoming a person.

The idea that life is an asset, and that we deserve freedom and happiness, is transmitted by belief in this. All our future progress is anticipated at home. Respect for the children provides the model for the respect they will have for others and for themselves. The arrival of another child teaches sharing, healthy competition, to love generously and to *value oneself.*

This is not instilled with rehearsed phrases, but with a general attitude. What is called *climate.*

What is the climate that governs in our home?

If our attitude should be of general distrust, there will be no words, little games or therapies that will persuade the child that to love is not fatal, that trust is possible, and even that the arrival of a sibling could be a bargain.

The atmosphere in which he lives will show him if it is good to have a family, to have brothers and sisters, friends, lovers, if it is worth it – if it is possible to love and respect without being betrayed.

Living together causes problems and frictions, but also joy and personal growth. Is there going to be jealousy between siblings? There will be. This too is normal, and is a foretaste of future relationships.

Sharing may be wretched, may be disagreeable: who would not want everything for himself: toys, parents, the home, the whole world? But sharing strengthens self-esteem and ability to interact. It is positive, but must be demonstrated as such. None of this demands great study or financial resources. It demands dedication, it demands tact, it demands tenderness: the minimum that someone born of us can expect.

~

Our real legacy to the children is not the house, not the bank account, and not even their studies, as our grandparents used to say.

The true treasure on which they are going to sustain themselves (or from which they will have to free themselves) is the message we pass to them every day. It is not in words chosen for special moments. It is not made up of Christmas nights or birthday parties, or the hour of sermonising or eulogy.

Such phrases as the following cast a veil of suspicion before their eyes:

'You need a brother. That'll teach you to be less selfish!'

'When your brother is born, all this easy-going will come to an end.'

'It's a good thing you're going to school next year, you'll learn some discipline.'

'When you grow, you'll see what is right; enjoy the time you have now when all you have to do is play.'

'When you marry and have children, then you'll certainly be nostalgic for when you were a child.'

'I would really like it if you were already married with lots of children, to see how painful regret is . . .'

Are we emotionally so low that affections are a burden? Do we really feel and think like that, have so mean an emotional range – or do we believe that it is educative to threaten? And if this was how we were taught, what do we do to correct this shortcoming?

Worse: much more than the words, we speak in the gesture, the voice, the look, the chemistry we give off. This is what governs in our room, our bed, our home, our meal table – the aura that distinguishes people and groups: affection or intolerance, partnership or disloyalty.

Frictions are part of reality and are certainly less harmful than pretence. What is hidden under the carpet is a tumour – the more fatal because concealed. All relationships must be realigned now and then, even in painful fragments.

However I am among those who believe that beyond and above this, loving is possible, at least loving more, loving better – loving with joy. The people who love us – and whom we love – are not necessarily beautiful, healthy, attractive. This also applies to parents and children.

Not everyone who has offspring likes children.

This is not a personality defect or a sign of perversity.

Some people when they take a child into their arms for the first time experience a whole panoply of unfamiliar feelings, which suddenly flood over them and bring enrichment.

For others iron enters the soul with some embraces. But there are others who were simply not born to be mother or father, although they can readily tolerate other affections.

These people, *men and women* (since we are not merely bundles of instincts), do not have the emotional equipment for that. Or they in their turn were not taught to love when they were little.

~

'Daddy, look there! How pretty! Stop the car; can I pick some flowers for Granny?'

The little girl picked yellow and violet wild flowers, and pinned them on her neck during the journey, eyes shining with delight. When they arrived, she ran to hand them to her grandmother.

The latter, in a spontaneous but sincere gesture, recoiled and remarked callously, 'Throw those out, those roadside flowers are dirty and have small insects that bite us!'

I shall never forget the look on that child's face.

The woman who displayed such coldness was not a bad person. She was not lacking in affection. However her confidence in things and people must have been shaken when she too was a small girl with armfuls of flowers for some adult of a desiccated disposition.

'You were born by accident; obviously I love you, but I never wanted children,' or 'I wanted to have just your brother, but your father wanted to try for a girl,' are blows, not to the face but to self-esteem.

Some people should not overload themselves emotionally by begetting children. I am no believer in slavish affection or slaves; what is essential to me might be expendable or a burden for someone else. Nor that he or I are better or worse. Having children does not ensure a union more or less worthwhile.

Because we think we must, because the family calls for it, because society expects it, because the spouse dreamed of this, because we demand come what may – even without specially liking the idea – we have a child.

Then, heaven knows why (through 'carelessness', to cement the marriage, to sort things out, to fill the vacuum), we have one or two more. The scene is set for an emotional collapse which swirls like spirals in water when an unyielding stone is thrown into it.

When I spoke of my joy because twin girls were born in my house, I was told in reproachful tones: 'So you want to be an old woman who takes care of the grandchildren?'

Another reaction from some people to whom we told the news, a spontaneous and therefore genuine manifestation, was negative: 'Twins? Two? What a handful! There goes your rest! Ah, your poor daughter! And their sister, is there a lot of jealousy already?'

Tasks and joys were doubled. True. Jealousy is the natural feeling of any child on whose birthday appear *competitors* and *companions*. Not necessarily *enemies*. But it is normal to have siblings, and the child is happy if the home is happy. By having siblings, any child in a sensible environment is being prepared to share, respect others and assert himself without seeking to destroy the other person.

Even today, when the twins are already several months old, people sometimes ask, 'And their poor sister, how is she turning out?'

I, who observe her daily, would say that she will turn out very well. As a child in a loving and fairly calm atmosphere, she solves the 'problem' in various ways. This appears in enchanting attitudes such as:

She won as a present a hair adornment with two identical dolls.

Someone asked, 'Are they little sisters?'

Her reply: 'No, these are my mummy and me.'

We had bought big rag dolls to decorate the two cradles. The sister grabbed one of them and for a day or two carried it about with her. When asked, she said, 'Mummy bought a doll for me and one for Fernanda, but she forgot about Fabiana, but she's going to buy one soon.'

We did not rebuke, or contradict. She was guarding in her universe the place that would belong to every child, with the certainty that hers was not the last in line and would not be seriously threatened. After a while she gave up the doll to her sister's cradle and returned to her usual toys.

For the moment the activity of this home requires adjustments, especially for a little girl aged four. At the same time we are dealing with two small lives full of demands. Sometimes all the women of the house surround the two pushchairs like fairies in a fairy tale, to admire, love, succour.

I have photos of my work table with a baby's bottle next to the computer, or two pushchairs with babies asleep beside the desk where I write.

Obligation, nuisance?

A loving choice.

Not because I am a good person or even a very conventional grandmother. But because for all of us it is a period of work and enchantment, and we practise more warmth, patience and reflection.

In the balance of days certainly joy weighs much more than all the rest, and ties of affection are being formed that time will not lessen.

In the family scenario I hope to be what I always wanted: a vulnerable and complicated but loving human being, who is tolerant of others. With all my errors, failings and obsessions, I value ties and affection, and I am brightened by this feeling that it is, after all, worthwhile.

I do not live thinking that at any moment someone is going to betray me. I am often afraid. I frequently make mistakes. I might crush someone I love, and certainly irrationally I sometimes feel myself wounded.

All the small human dramas are mine. Over the years and multiple affections, more than once when I thought there would be a celebration, it was a fiasco. When I imagined an encounter, it was loneliness. When I wanted an embrace, I was shunned.

Or much of this did happen and was beautiful, and good, and exceeded my expectations.

But here, in this area of ancestral family affections – that has been constrained by the tempo and conditions of modern life – I go on gaining rather than losing. In the hope that within the petty or great storms that occur for all of us, there may remain a memory of hope, of love and loyalty.

An angel comes to visit

The man was picking up the keys of the car (the woman had already left to take the children to school) when there was a ring at the bell.

Slightly irritated, because he was already rather late, he opened the door: 'Yes?'

A lanky unknown youth, androgynous, handsome and ugly, tall and short, black and blond, made a small signal by bending the index finger: 'I've come to fetch you.'

No explanation was needed, the man understood: the Angel of Death was there, and there was no escape. But accustomed to negotiation and even in his perturbation quickly realising that it was early, too early, he tried to argue: 'But how come? Now, like this, with no warning or anything? No decent deadline?'

The Angel smiled a generous and perverse smile, sighed and said: 'Isn't there anybody with the originality to welcome me with sympathy in this world? Is nobody ever ready? It is true that you are only 40, but even at 80 they object.'

The man held more firmly to the car key, which he had at last located in his coat pocket, and persisted: 'Come on, give me a chance.'

The Angel took pity; this person was really afraid. Oh, humans . . . Then he had a rush of goodwill and conceded: 'All right. I'll give you a chance, if you give me three good reasons why you should not come with me this time.'

(Was there a sly gleam in the blue and black eyes of that Angel?)

The man stood upright; obviously, he knew that he would hit the target, he had always been a good negotiator. But when he opened his mouth to begin his litany of reasons (far more than three, oh yes) the Angel raised an imperious finger.

'Hold on. Three good reasons, but it is not worth saying that your business must be sorted, your family is not taken care of, your wife does not know how to sign a cheque, your children know nothing of reality. What matters is you, yourself. Why would it be worthwhile to leave you here a bit longer?'

~

I was told this fable and I have already retold it in another book, in which the person who opened the door was a woman. The objection the angel made to her before she could begin to recite her reasons was: '*It is not worth saying "because your husband and children need you"* . . .'

This little story speaks of how much we are worth *for ourselves*, how much we are worth *by ourselves*, what we really feel and think *about ourselves*.

Someone, who was coolly aware of his limitations and his achievements, told me:

'If today at the age of 61 I should meet the idealistic lad I was at 18, I should not be ashamed to shake his hand, and could look him straight in the eye without having to avert my gaze.'

He made this comment without a scrap of solemnity or self-glorification, but in good humour, and with a gentle irony in regard to himself that is not contempt but love.

How many of us can say that? What arguments could we use to persuade the visiting angel not to take us away yet? The story presents a good reason for us to reflect on the passage of time and our growth as human beings.

How can we programme ourselves or invest our share of humanity in a personal project that makes sense?

It gives us good reason for thinking of the *value of having values*, taking the measure of life, not just skimming over the surface. Do we from time to time interrupt our activity for this purpose – or are we overwhelmed by the agitation of the media, fashion, and consumerism, and the race for a higher salary, a better position, a smarter table in the restaurant, a craftier method of fooling someone else and rising, even if in a small way, from our meanest position?

'Ah, I follow my values.'

'I taught my values to my children.'

We employ this term too readily. Which values? Those according to which I try to live, expressed not in a chance sermon or talk, but in the way I live my routine in the family, at work, with friends, with my loves?

I am conscious that by loving ourselves more we can live better, and we can deal with this. We begin by trying to change perspective: instead of seeing just the wall in front, observe a piece of the landscape. Going from victim to author of oneself is a useful step.

Maturing helps in the task of seeing reality better, and it is not a disaster. Reading helps. Opening one's eyes to the beautiful and positive helps. Loving and being loved helps. Therapy helps. At least, it will help us to keep our head above water instead of drowning ourselves in self-pity.

Reinventing oneself totally is impossible: the contour of these boundaries, the terrain of which they are made is established. We carry a stamp on the soul – but we can redefine its shape. Perhaps change colours here, or open a clearing there and build a shelter.

3

Taming to avoid being devoured

Much will depend on how much we expect and believe.

Generally speaking, I think that we content ourselves with very little. I am not talking of money, car, house, clothing, jewellery, travel, for which we yearn increasingly. I am referring to human treasures: ethics, loyalty, friendship, love, refined sensuality.

Our wings are not so shaky that we must fly close to the ground or just drag our weight. Nor are we such cowards that we cannot poke our head out of the cocoon and look around: perhaps in the time we are fleeing a ready harvest of attributes – future, confidence, project, life – awaits us.

Although people may not even notice, everything is an advance and transformation, an accumulation of experience, the birth pangs of ourselves, every day remade.

We are better than we think we are.

In the mirror placed before us at the hour of our birth, people in the end have projected more than a void, a nothing, a frustration: a full countenance is reflected, perhaps a whole landscape seen from the porticoes of our soul.

No need for consensus
nor art,
nor beauty nor age,
life is always within
and now.
(Life is mine
to be dared.)

Life can flourish
in an entire existence.
But must be sought after, must be
conquered.

The geisha in the corner of the room

Years ago when I was already considering the particular themes of this book, I decided to organise women's groups for us to discuss the topic 'Maturity: Losses and Gains'.

I invited a friend who was an experienced therapist to take part. Though they would not be therapeutic groups, I should be dealing, more directly than in books and lectures, with this singular creature called the human soul. I would not wish to have to improvise at possible crisis moments.

We proposed to bring together at most ten women and let them exchange ideas and experiences on the theme of maturing. At each meeting we would suggest an aspect of the theme or ask for their suggestions. It was quite informal. Anyone who wanted, who felt like it, would give her testimony or express her ideas on some topic. Everyone could comment and discuss.

Taming to avoid being devoured

Today let us talk of our fears.

Our regrets, our delights.

Our dreams and plans.

The suggestion could come like that, direct, in a phrase, or in some text they were given to read. The primary intention was to discover: Who am I or think I am, and who do I want to be, who would I like to be?

Why do we waste so much energy trying to be what we are not, cannot be – perhaps have no real desire to be?

Does it also depend on me? If it does, to what extent does it mean that I like myself? Do I want to be happy, healthy, loving, lapped in affection or do I really want to be resentful and bitter? Is this 'my nature'?

Or if I want to change: how do I change, how do I face up to the effects of change?

As happens among women, the climate was almost immediately one of dialogue and understanding. Some shy, others extrovert, more reserved or forthcoming, they soon took charge of the debates, sometimes in confidential tones, at other times, in real discussions. Tears, laughter. Amazement: 'You too! I thought that I was the only one like that. I thought that nobody had this problem.'

Nothing particularly intimate, only manifestations that provoked much reflection among us as we left the meetings. Certainly we learned with these women that they were doing the best they could for themselves: they wanted to understand, wanted to change, wanted to be happier.

~

Their ages varied from 40 to 80, the majority in their 50s, and all were liberal professionals or 'housewives' of searching intelligence – indispensable for any debate. They were of the generation of pioneers that we all are: we do not have precedents to imitate nor even to breach, given that the universe of our mothers is in some aspects so incomparably distant from our own.

Most difficult was seeing how much, regardless of occupation, we still put ourselves down. Insecurity appeared to be our brand, uncertainty as to what we were worth and could make of ourselves (not only 'should').

Years, decades, centuries of cultural preconceptions still held us, despite all the innovations. What did we need?

First, discernment.

Emotions were muddled. There was uncertainty and discontent, but the women could not even allow themselves to explain this clearly. A moral unease had brought them all to that room. How to act in relation to it?

It was important to define it better. By talking, as it happens – since by putting a name to things we begin to have control over them – there were defined spaces of interrogation, revealing contours. Our ill-being took shape.

One of the most important aspects was how shadowy the line was between love and servitude. Between generosity and self-destruction. Between adaptation and self-harm.

For any change it is necessary to understand what has gone wrong in our loving relationship, in our home, work . . . in us. In what were we victims, how far did we collaborate in this situation? *What* can I do, *how* can I do it, can I *still* do it?

$\sim$

A word spoken, a text read can make us perceive what should be obvious but is not: because it is too disturbing it is better left hidden under all the carpets of our resignation.

We go about with the knowledge that love should not be servitude. That at any age we could count on ourselves. That it is possible to open new doors and if necessary to break down some around and within us.

We should take on decisions, institute a new personal order, review contracts and sign agreements. Much of this was not articulated among the women, but was tacit. Much would have to be discussed, eventually fought over in the family or wherever.

A new way of being was possible, and this was disturbing. There were some who asked whether it might not be preferable for everything to stay as it was before those meetings: in the normality of the accepted routine and the truncated dream.

'Now, what should we do?' they exclaimed, with enthusiasm or apprehension.

Each would do or not do what might be better, more sensible, viable. For some the sole possibility would be to let everything stay as it was. For all, however, nothing would ever be the same again: questioning the established, even though it might not eventually be changed, was a way of feeling that they were alive.

~

The central question was always the loving relationship. With parents for some, with offspring for many, the companionship with the partner for virtually all.

Women who wasted themselves on relationships that inhibited or sapped their talents were educated to please, not to exercise tenderness, but to carry out roles and duties: a very shaky basis for positive interaction with colleagues, friends, husband or offspring.

The constantly available mother and the submissive wife, even the eternally solicitous colleague or official provoke guilt and hostility in others. Life is spent in a double loneliness: of the one who surrenders and of the one who subjugates against their will. Living together does not become dialogue or partnership, but a frustrating dual monologue.

Changing this would be almost a miracle for many people. However, there lurks potential for previously unimagined achievement for each, or for the two partners together.

Changing anything, whether it be the hairstyle or the usual place at the table, is difficult. For anyone more destructured it could be a battle with many wounds across the board.

Feeling treated unjustly is crushing, but conformity can be beguilingly comfortable:

'There is nothing to be done, that's the way I am. My parents, my husband, my fate were tyrants. It's too late now.'

The harm that others did to us – or we did to ourselves – makes accusing sentinels at our gate. The trick is to try to take control of these ghosts so that they do not manipulate us. Some disagreements are cleared up with a good conversation, even years later, and we may be surprised at how often the instigator of this suffering had not noticed anything untoward.

Other scars are irremovable, they are permanent, they leave us misshapen. For these, goodwill, gentleness with oneself, wisdom and acceptance (I did not use the term 'resignation' since I do not like it) are required.

Many women regretted what they had done or left undone years before: the wrong choices, the omissions, resignation and subservience; insecurity, doubts; premature marriages, important decisions taken thoughtlessly, serious responsibilities shouldered when one was still so immature.

One had given up work because she had children and the husband did not want them to be left with a nursemaid. Another abandoned studying for a master's degree because the children were complaining about her absence from home. Another was not able to go to university because her father wanted his daughters at home. One of them might have been able to take a doctorate in another state, but could not bring herself to mention this wish since her husband 'would have been angry'.

One admitted that she had not wanted children because she had little maternal feeling; her real desire was to shine in a profession that thrilled her but only now that her children were grown up could she really carry on satisfactorily.

So why did she have children, three in fact? Well, because it was what girls did, what husbands and parents expected. That's how it was.

In recounting these old facts they seemed like girls caught misbehaving merely for daring to have such desires. One or the other smiled, shaking her head: 'Heavens, what a fool I was.'

~

They were models of good and dedicated women who in a relationship – more than just lovers or friends – were submissive to masculine stereotypes. The loneliness of their men was certainly as immense as this inequality.

We suggested that each in her own way should carry out a review of these processes. Why had they acted in one way or another? What could they do, now, so many years later, in this regard?

'I can't do anything now,' was the reaction of one. 'It happened twenty years ago, it's over, there's no point.'

The tendency is to keep dragging along these small corpses, the 'if only I had . . . if he had . . .'

I can go round this fissure by pretending there is no problem; lie down beside it, weeping; bury myself in it with my skills and hopes; cover it over with leaves, branches, planks, pretending that nothing happened. Try to fill this negative balance with something positive, that in each case will be peculiar to the individual. Demand why I acted in that way at that moment. Was it through ignorance, cowardice, an urge to self-destruct?

In the comparative clarity of maturity we can see that most of these 'pitfalls' become less disastrous with the realisation: '*At that moment, in those circumstances, I did my best.*' Almost always there was a reason: small children, the partner's problems, genuine difficulty in actually leaving home or town, social or family pressure – factors not always negative. Only realities with which one tried to deal as one could at the time.

Gradually old problems were faced with more clarity: on that occasion I did the best I could, although today, in maturity, I see that I could have acted differently. In that phase, when still immature, I could not, my parents did not understand, my husband did not know.

Maturity contributes to this: a new view, in the light of a certain distancing, enables us to understand hitherto obscure factors of our own and of others. Sometimes a kind of amnesty is provided. On that basis patterns can be rearranged.

I like to use the word *amnesty* – rather than pardon – since it does not carry a religious connotation, nor does it give the idea that we are saints offering forgiveness.

Not even to ourselves.

~

One day I suggested that we should talk openly about what aroused our anger.

At first nobody responded to this: all had a marvellous husband, the finest children, saintly parents, a ban on feelings of anger. Suddenly one woman, who rarely spoke, began softly: 'I feel anger. I feel huge anger.'

Her anger was over an invalid mother who tortured her with the tyranny of the weak, of some sick people and of very spoiled children. Another woman then said she had anger over the sacrifices she made for two adult sons who still lived with her; they were always dissatisfied and bad-mannered. One criticised herself for feeling anger over a husband who paid her no heed or regard. ('For him it seems I don't exist, I am not even human.') Others felt great anger for the choices made in youth, of which I have spoken above.

The list was long and lively.

We began to discover that to feel anger (not spite) could be healthy and necessary. Never to feel anger – this was not talking about hatred or resentment – is to lie to oneself.

Many of these reasons for anger can be seen from another angle: to submit to bad-mannered sons is the result of a whole process, from birth or before, in which the mother needs to feel a victim, self-righteous – the martyr. Kicking over the traces, climbing off that high horse (or pedestal) may provoke an admirable transformation in a relationship. Certainly husband and offspring ought to experience a mixture of anger and guilt in relation to that spouse-mother-martyr.

When things seem really a mess, a friend taught me, one can ask oneself: 'Is it a tragedy or only a nuisance?'

In the great majority of cases it is a nuisance. An overdue account, a stupid boss, a jealous colleague, an insolent child, a taciturn husband, a fractious elderly mother, five kilos overweight – just frustrations. Excessive rain, excessive sun. Great cold, great heat: suddenly every time we draw breath, it seems the end of the world.

A good clear-out in the storerooms of the heart brings great relief: we throw out the nuisances or we lay them aside for a while, and we move on to dealing with serious matters.

Gradually we find that we breathe easier. We can even dream.

~

Diminished self-esteem, companion to insecurity and fear, will point us to many mistaken choices in youth. It would trap many of us even now in a fateful pattern bringing unease into the family atmosphere, and continual personal suffering.

If we undervalue ourselves, not only do we tend to keep things as they are (better the devil you know than the devil you don't), but we take – or do not take – decisions out of fear. Fear of loneliness, of being unable to decide on our own, fear of the opinion of others, fear.

Anyone who underestimates herself needs someone at her side to confirm her worth as a human being. In this situation there is no dialogue, since the even balance is too damaged. It is surprising the difficulty women, even capable ones, have in feeling themselves justified, worthy in their own right.

'I do not seem complete without a companion, without at least thinking and saying, "I have someone,"' a woman lawyer told me.

Even among women who are highly successful in their personal and professional lives will there be someone who is afraid of being on her own, who flourishes under someone else's shadow and believes her true vocation is to serve, to please, to provide: *the geisha*.

The latter is resistant to all the innovations and conquests of our time.

'A man likes a woman who cannot choose from the menu or pretends she cannot and lets him decide,' a young woman told me in a (passing) phase of disillusion. But perhaps we are not much good at choosing a companion even for a dinner date? And who says that a man with this taste will be able to value us, however interesting he is?

Take care: a man appreciative of the prattling of a geisha and his favourite meal always ready might be masculine and powerful, but he runs the risk of becoming a eunuch – in his emotions, which will be very constrained.

~

Although our ambivalence makes everything more interesting through the multiplicity of options and interpretations, it does on the other hand trap us on the seesaw of indecision. We suffer this dichotomy between 'wanting' to do and what we think we 'must' do. We implement in ourselves the phrase from our infancy that I heard ceaselessly: *Children should not want*.

In some respects we remain children – enjoying the privileges and suffering the constraints of that condition. Anyone who lives with us, husband or offspring, will take on extra baggage, which will cosset him or leave him alone: having alongside him the eternal small girl on whom nobody can rely, with whom he cannot really share life.

Money and education do not give us an easy escape from the secular brainwashing of our culture. Nobody casts down boundary walls by passivity. And the presupposition ('culture') suggests to us that it is the man's role to be active. We women must be gentle, conciliatory, agreeable, seductive, arousing in the man feelings of power and protection, and take continual charge of the offspring to show how dedicated we are.

In short, we must prove that we *deserve* affection.

We are created in the light of the hypothetical saving principle that will determine – and must at all costs manage – our future. And naturally it will treat us as children. We shall always be the dispossessed, without scope or strength for decision. We shall belong to our parents, then to the husband, children and grandchildren.

Our share will be the corner of the dining room table left over when we want to write, the son's computer when we venture onto the Internet, the sofa with the other women at the dinners of married couples.

At our back looms the terror of time passing and devouring

an existence we may never learn to handle – since it never belonged to us. Worse: we may not even want to handle it because this would mean abandoning resigned protection for the shock of decisions; facing obstacles and at last exercising the so fondly desired – and feared – power over ourselves.

When that angel should come to knock on our door offering the chance of not taking us yet if we can give three good reasons why not, what shall we have to tell him beyond the usual excuses: 'Husband and children need me, and I haven't yet cleaned the house,' or 'I must do the shopping and make the dinner'?

Do not fool yourselves: what I am saying was not only happening at the beginning of the past century, and today does not occur only among the less informed and simple women. The situation of men and women – since if I speak of the latter I am inevitably involving the former – is much evolved but continues in full mutation.

Much remains to be done for it to become possible to talk of genuine partnership. It demands a balance: there is no dialogue between servant and master.

~

A frequent complaint in our meetings was – nothing new – the absence of dialogue with husbands and lovers.

'But did you attempt dialogue, did you try sometimes to converse with your husband, your lover, your son even?'

'Oh, it's no use . . . men don't like to talk . . . they have difficulty with words, don't have the knack . . . they run away from emotion . . . they are cowards. It's in their nature.'

Is that the case?

Or do we prevent our men from talking because we demand too much, demand that they should be like us, should speak our language – instead of the language of men?

Do we really provide scope for them on our side, do we really encourage them, are we partners? Or when they come home do we drench them with a mass of complaints about the house, the children, the traffic, the supermarket prices – as if this, our immediacy, were the only reality?

It is not impossible for people who speak different tongues to understand each other: through mime, expression, look, tone of voice, soul and body and a *liking* that transmits all of that.

There should not be only a string of woes and complaints, but we should share many moments of laughter and good humour. Something was said above of the importance of good humour in living together, in living, in taking positive enjoyment from all the transformations: 'At some moments it is not love that saves us,' a friend told me, 'it is humour.'

Good humour is an attractive quality and a wise attitude.

It is not a matter of sarcasm, of making fun at the expense of others, but of laughing at oneself at the right moment, respecting and loving oneself, but not regarding oneself as always unjustly treated and under attack.

It can be a last resort: 'Either I try to smile, even at myself, or I cut my wrists,' someone with cause for despair said to me. And he smiled at me, like someone saying: I shall succeed, people will succeed, it is in the end worthwhile.

I cannot make a joke when I lose a lover or a friend, when I discover that I am ill or I lose my job. Good humour does not mean jokes: it is the affectionate smile, the loving silence, the welcoming shoulder open for someone else and for me.

Our evolution, the impositions of our group and culture, our own fantasies, demand much energy and determination plus a pinch of good humour to be tamed – and to not devour us unceremoniously and pitilessly.

~

We had in mind a brief spell of work with women only.

But after nearly a year of successive groups, when we were already thinking of suspending the work because of pressure of other engagements, there was a list of ten men who wanted to take part. So we made a final group, this time of men only.

'Why were they not mixed?' we are always asked.

Because we had no idea how far this would go. From our wish to bring together one or two groups, merely because I wanted to take the pulse of women, we reached more than ten. I never intended to bring men together with women, since we had only four meetings each time, and there would not be long enough to establish the desired spontaneity.

I was curious what the men would say on the matter of losses and gains of maturity.

The men's group had results strikingly similar to those of the women: they questioned their choices, resented ageing, suffered from the fear of losing their potency (both economic power and authority), of losing their health and body shape. They were also incensed that though they were exhausted it seemed impossible to stop or reduce the rhythm of work: wives and offspring were too dependent on them.

They were burdened with concern for their offspring and guilt from thinking that they had failed in the family: they could have had more dialogue, dedication and tolerance. Many felt isolated within their own home. The peculiar link between mother and offspring excluded them.

'The children come to me only to ask for money,' one of them bemoaned. 'When they want friendship, to talk of personal things, they look for their mother.'

Their children's hearts, even those of the boys, was terrain on to which they could not go directly. From early on they had been taught that the man was an intruder in the territory of a mother and her offspring.

'Careful, you're going to let the baby fall! A man is not as adept with a child. Let me take care of this, you can read your newspaper, watch your football.'

These are not phrases I made up just now but ones that were spoken by many of us to those whom we would later accuse of being 'remote' from the children. Do we perhaps do this to be the sole possessors of what we regard as our only genuine asset, our most personal 'object', our product, born of us – 'our' child?

Women build walls around their relationship with the child and leave the man outside. Naturally they will spend their life complaining that he took no interest in the baby, did not know what to do with the children.

~

The loneliness of men seemed to me more barren than that of women, who have other kinds of affective links: family, friends, even their house.

'The young men, my colleagues,' one university woman told me, 'when they chat among themselves describe assets, they talk of money, football, politics and women. We girls (some were already married), when we are together, we share secrets or we moan (about mothers, children, household chores, or about men).'

Men retreat into silence, between the superficial chat of their male friends and the fear of disappointing or shocking (or annoying?) women with their frailty, more intimate concerns or dramas.

With their women often querulous, obsessively enclosed in their motherhood, busy with domestic chores or in excessive futility, men are left with the role of provider. The need for someone with whom they could exchange ideas, to whom they could really open up, was almost a constant in their comments: 'With my friends, I talk about the things men talk about: politics, football; with my wife, I don't want to open up because she soon gets upset and taxes me with a thousand things; as for the children, well I have to protect them, don't I?'

There are nearly always things to improve, and nearly always they can be improved. There is no bar on questioning, clarifying, explaining. There is no shame in fulfilling the dream of studying, opening a shop, taking a journey, changing one's occupation. Changing a relationship.

It is easier to give up: to die before one's time. Cross and elderly married couples or young married couples alone in the house are terribly sad and terribly common.

'When I am depressed, getting up from bed (and not creeping around the house) is already an act of heroism,' someone remarked. Living is heroism, living well a long love affair is even more heroic. Living alone if my love affair has failed is a battle for sheer survival.

However, is just keeping one's head above water in a marriage sufficient?

A friend on his wife's birthday said one of the most beautiful things I have heard:

'Every day of our marriage [some 40 years] I chose you anew as my wife.'

The happiest married couple must be one that does not stop chasing the dream that, despite grief, people should see each other each day as on the first day, should *focus on themselves* – and should choose anew.

~

I was asked one day to write on the '*perfect couple*': good for someone who likes challenges. My first precaution was to put quotation marks around the word 'perfect'.

What would justify the label I should write about?

It occurred to me immediately that partners in a 'perfect' couple need to wish each other well as they wish well to good friends, and temper this affection with the sensuality that distinguishes friendship from love. Two people who, without resentment or demands, understand the inescapable ingredients of the human being and the communication barrier. In the final analysis, all the complications.

The best partnership must be one where each partner accepts the other without having to submit to the other in *anything*; where each values and admires the other, but with a feeling of tenderness and care. Above all, where each partner does not invest *all* their plans in the other, and at the first disappointment turns from love to hatred.

If the other is to serve as a peg for our most extravagant dreams of perfection, the first contrary wind will fell the wretched idol who is guilty of nothing.

In a healthy marriage there is a general proposition: I want to spend the rest of my days with you, build a significant, definitive and attractive relationship with you.

It is important not to rush to the other's arms in flight from the annoyances of the family, the ring of loneliness, the ache of boredom. It is essential not to throw oneself on someone else's neck by falling into the trap of 'at last never alone again!' because a union with exaggerated expectations is destined to be the start of exile.

A good love affair, more than anything, must endure and triumph over the daily living together.

The bill to be paid, the sick son, the daughter with a complex, the mother with Alzheimer's, the father in depression, or the thankless job and the uncouth boss. When the last straw comes – and it may be the most trivial straw – people explode. They want to kill and die, and take heed: nothing more in our relationship is how it was at the beginning. It is a long way from what we planned.

We do not want to go on like this, but we do not know what to do. Or we know, but it seems to us impossible to put into effect.

In truth, in the loving partnership as in everything else we must start from scratch every day. Then we can try a new start here and now. The routine comfort, its small rituals are the signs of our more secure life, but they also bring disenchantment and monotony.

It is said that we need creativity in a loving relationship. The trouble is that when one talks of 'creativity' in a relationship, most people think at once of innovations in the sex act, as if the solution were in new positions, another perfume, exotic artifices.

Good love-making is a result, not a means. Just as offspring should be: fruit of a living affection, not an instrument to repair what has failed.

After the first phase of passion has passed (forgive me, but it passes, which does not imply boredom or the end of pleasure), we begin to love in another way. Or the love is better; or *here is where we begin to love*; to wish well; to appreciate; to respect; to value; to court; to miss; to allow scope; to want the other to grow and not remain clinging.

'*If you love someone, leave him free,*' was written on a small note – one of the greatest gifts from someone among so many other fine things.

A little clarity and a touch of maturity (what a great thing time is) must show if something – and what – can still be conquered as a pair.

When this is understood, the moment for definition has come: and now, what to do? Invest, if there are options other than a void.

As we do not easily give up – because we are, after all, fighters or we should no longer be here, and because there are children, obligations, house, investment and even affection – we are going to try the trick of rebuilding what appears smashed. That is when there is a will, affection, a surviving interest. So long as there is a reinvention as a pair, not the surrender of one and the exile of the other, since the space between the oppressor and the oppressed is a void.

What if nothing really remains on the positive side?

Ties can be reconstituted, patched up or cut. The cut is made with more or less generosity and warmth or hostility and anger – always with pain. However, no union should be a categorical sentence of mutual destruction within a cage.

~

Since I make up stories, I like fables.

I work with them because they are the mirror of reality. And because I like stories about angels, here is another one. It tells of love, partnership in love, of finding who can be our accomplice, far beyond and above conventions, formulas and 'fashions'.

There was a man, an ordinary man, whom a mundane fate seemed to control totally. A well-trained domestic animal.

One day he felt a discomfort in both shoulders – muscle strain, poor posture at work . . . It was getting worse and he decided to take a look at himself in the mirror, from the side, and entirely naked after his bath. There was no doubt, two oblique bumps were visible on his skin under the shoulders. He was afraid but decided not to say anything to anybody, and, as he did not often have sex with his wife, he managed to hide everything for almost a month.

He did what he had seen his wife do: he grabbed from above the basin a round mirror in which she primped her hair, and began to study all day the phenomenon that instead of frightening him now intrigued him. Curious, but without suffering – for it did not hurt – he was watching it grow.

And he was thinking: No use going to the doctor, for if it were a tumour (or two) that large, there was no further cure, and better to die whole than to be cut up.

On an occasion when he was masturbating in the bathroom, he felt at the moment of pleasure that the bumps were launching from his back, and he saw himself adorned with them, folded like the wings of a swan that had just been asleep and, on waking, would wallow in the water.

He stood there, naked in front of the mirror, astounded.

Now he was not merely an ordinary man with bills to pay, a job to do, family to maintain, children to take to the park, working hours to keep: he was a man with an enchantment.

These wings were very practical, because so long as he wore a fairly loose shirt they fitted wonderfully under his clothes. On some nights, when everyone was asleep, he would go out to the terrace, strip and beat the air.

His wife noticed something different in her husband's body. He was becoming bent: so many hours at the work table. Nothing more than that. Although her mother had told her that 'with a man it is always better to doubt', she had never imagined anything very unusual of her tame husband.

'This way you will end up a hunchback. Stand up straight,' she would say in her tone of conjugal disapproval.

Things became complicated when, already accustomed to his new condition, the man-angel looked around and, being still only a man with wings, felt very alone. And he began to think about this. And he looked around and fell in love.

On the first night with his lover, he forgot the problem, took off all his clothes, and when she began to stroke his back the pair of wings opened, and arched by joining the tips high up above him at the moment of highest pleasure.

But this woman/lover was not afraid, did not back away. She opened more to him, and said: 'Come with me, come with me, come with me . . .'

And she opened her wings as well.[1]

~

Love is a complex task, above all because *for me to love it is necessary first to love myself.* Inside and outside are mutual reflexes, like two mirrors on opposite sides. I am seeking a love good for me – in which I recognise me and rediscover me, remake me and broaden me, explore me, lay myself open – if my interior image will allow.

Love more than anything *reveals us*: demonstrates our tendencies, what we prefer and what we choose for ourselves. Do I want and deserve to be happy and do happy things, or do I need to punish myself and castigate another; am I deserving and capable of growth or am I destroying myself – and the other with me?

Loving 'choice' may seem a contradiction. In the old days the talk was of 'choosing a husband, choosing a wife'. I always had great doubts about this. Today I think it is a choice, yes, but not the one to which such advice referred: it is a matter of choosing well your husband, your wife. The idea, explicit or not, was that the husband should give you economic security, that the wife should be virtuous and take good care of the home and the children.

[1] Lya Luft, *Histórias do Tempo*, Sao Paulo: Ediciones Siciliano e Mandarin, 2000

This speaks of arrangements and convenience, or rigid models imposed from outside. Love is another kind of choice. The man with wings came upon his winged lover, apparently by chance: it was in truth his most vital choice of a partner.

This encounter occurs in the dark of mutual unknowing. It is conscious in part, according to our pleasure and needs, the plan we have, the model we want. But it is quite unconscious, springs from impulses more primary than that *I* of ours hidden behind many masks.

This is the most serious option: it stems from the entire interior perspective. *In the choice of a partner I opt for what I judge I deserve.* That is where we may stab ourselves in the chest.

I choose according to my emotional health or my sickness, my darkest desires, my unconscious movements in the direction of affirmation or destruction.

On our most hidden side it sits, scents: here I must invest my emotion, here I can give myself, here is someone with whom I can think of building a relationship.

~

In love we think we can finally live the myth of fusion with the other. We want to lose identity in the hands of someone who for the moment is 'everything' for us.

The initial passion wants to see and be seen. It is the compulsion to open up to the other and to drown in him, revealing the minutest details of our body and soul, unflagging tales of the past, exchanges that seem to lead to the dream of total union.

We know every minute of his timetable, to whom he is talking, where he is and intends or would dream to be at such and such a time – a manner of being always together, affirmation of affection and interest.

However, a loving liaison is a long elaboration: it faces a whole series of transformations across the board. We change and the partners do not necessarily change at the same rhythm, with the same intensity or with the same feeling.

Instinct and affection are what enable good couples, loving couples, to use these crisis phases to renew themselves and to grow, if possible, together. So long as the instinct is healthy, the affection good, the personality open.

There is no recipe. There is no school. There is no manual.

One of the partners will inevitably age earlier, be more prone to sickness. One can have financial reverses, professional failures. One can evolve with age and circumstances, or lag in relation to the other.

Between both is played a power game in which the weaker will tyrannise the one (not always the woman) who is more submissive, abdicates from more things.

Being vulnerable and essentially guilty, the one who has the advantage (whatever that may mean) may yield to blackmail, prune his wings and trim his destiny to avoid 'humiliating' the partner.

In the case of a woman, the drama is more complex, because it is our convention (perhaps a primitive legacy from the caves) that the man should be strong and the woman weak, the man the owner of the money (= power) and the woman who lives on the housekeeping. I know successful women who at the end of every month hand over the money for the husband to administer, because they feel incapable, or worse, are afraid that being capable leaves the husband insecure and aggressive.

Therapy for each of them, or as a pair, or for one of them at least, or counselling, could be an excellent tool. Holidays away from work and offspring, an opportunity for re-encounter and frank discussion. Most frequently the one who could take the decisive step and repair her life – even with this relationship – does not permit it. Guilt does not allow. The fear of losing the partner does not permit. The dread of loneliness is worse still.

Everything stays as it is: beneath the appearances runs the turgid river of slow and silent physical or moral suicide of the couple. It is the death of joys and tenderness, a fatal agreement in which hope is rescinded. Guilt, someone said, is like a suitcase full of bricks, useless weight we carry from one side to the other for no purpose. There can be only one solution: throw it all out, or part at least.

But self-imposed rules, agreements never spoken, adjustments apparently necessary to avoid a conflict that might be salutary – not to speak of the deaf war that develops so ceaselessly among couples – or expediency, prevent us from acting. They raise those impassable Pillars of Hercules that will be destroyed at some later moment with violence and pain, or will be a monument in honour of two proscribed existences.

～

Writing about love I cannot speak only of submissive women.

I know husbands so under the thumb of their partner that there is no room left for new friendships, or even for the simple exchange of ideas and support – still less if it were with another woman. In a house I frequented as a kid, the husband and the male children had to take off their shoes on reaching the front door: there were slippers awaiting the wretches. 'Don't come into my house with your dirty shoes!' would bawl the general in skirts who was in command.

The stifled personality dreams of escape. Eventually, if it appears and is more attractive, a rupture occurs, followed by the infallible comment of an outsider: 'But, how come? They seemed to get on so well!'

~

This is worth a postscript: the attraction outside the liaison of a union that has turned mortal does not need to be 'a third person', but an opportunity to grow, to travel, to study, to leave a job, to form a new friendship. To be able to be joyful, to be able to breathe. To be able to trust. Not to feel oneself under inspection or ignored. But we can opt to let everything be: *that's the way it is*.

Sometimes there really is no means of escape.

In that case, if that angel of darkness or light should knock at the door, we shall not be able to offer at least one good reason, of our own, why he should not take us, bringing closure to something that to tell the truth was already null and void.

Dancing with the scarecrow

I have said or hinted here that maturing should be seen as something positive and that ageing is not the annulment of individuality.

One of the reasons for our frustrations, as men and women, is that we live in a culture that idolises youth and deifies physical form above any sensibility.

If maturity is the fruit of youthfulness and old age is the result of maturity, living means a natural weaving of the web of existence. A process so deceptively simple for the one who is living it, so unusual for the one who is observing it. So insignificant in the context of human history.

Following this current, we navigate, decked out in our circumstances, carrying the baggage we were given and were acquiring. We choose part of the script, draw something on the margins, accompanied by positive presences but also by the demon of our difficulty in living well, always ready to do away with ourselves.

We do not always take charge of living: it forms part of our culture, our education, the media and personality. It is in the magazines, in the mentality of those around us and of those we love, it is within us. It grows and spreads insofar as we are not used to dealing with it.

The enemy is varied, has many heads. 'We are many,' said the devil in the Gospels who would possess an unfortunate. All these heads control and inhibit us: imposition and acceptance of intangible models; the non-valuation of self; submission to preconceptions; absence of personal values; frivolities in the most varied emotional relationships. The consequent dread of a process that instead of evolving and growing terrifies us as annihilation.

We must overcome the idea that we are merely running towards our end, in a process of deterioration and extinction.

This is our most destructive phantasm, since it is fed by our fear of death, and grows disproportionately because *our interior void allows it extraordinary scope.*

If we wish – more than to survive – to grow as thinking human beings, this bedside clock or wristwatch (especially the mental clock) must be just what it is: an instrument to measure and coordinate routine activities. To mark the phases with their enchantments and boundaries, their richness and their privations, with the general meaning of *growth, not mutilation.*

At every transition we carry out our rituals, we lose some assets and we gain others, some won with great effort. I am speaking of *interior assets.*

Assets that a bank closure or national bankruptcy will not exhaust; assets not lost even when the beloved dies; assets that cheer us in grief, help us in joy to seek more, and in boredom – when everything appears so pointless – to stir buried currents of energy below an apparently dead surface.

When we think it is all over, that we shall never again feel joy or emotion, everything that was hoarded and is good emerges at consequent full strength.

These are the treasures I am talking about: they can defeat what paralyses us. It requires us to overcome the culture of here and now: profit, acquisition, being on top, incessant making and mending.

Losses and Gains

In childhood everything is always now.

We are busy being alive.

Gradually a distinction is drawn between *before* and *after*, perhaps through temporary separation from a comforting presence that goes and returns in a still immeasurable time. Absence becomes real in a flash when the person comes back. 'Oh, weren't you there?'

Finally we emerge from those tepid waters and we perceive that we exist – in time. We are in a process, on a journey, we are en route.

Limbo becomes clear and our story begins.

As a small girl I liked to get up at daybreak and savour the forbidden, since a child should lie quietly in bed until her mother calls her. I would go to the window and open it, slowly to avoid making a noise. How magical the garden was at that hour. Full of the night that was ending, full of hope for the day that would begin.

Even at that stage I did not find the alternation of night and day hostile, but a kind of witchcraft that would provoke transformations: the cocoon with a promise of shining wings.

Why now, necessarily, with body enlarged, skin less smooth, wrinkles and experience, should I be in decline and not in a natural transformation – like anything else?

What is beautiful in a baby is displeasing in an adolescent. What dazzles in a youth may be out of place in a mature person. So old age – if it is not a caricature of youth – has its fitting charm.

~

'But what can be positive about being old?' I was asked one day. 'Tell me just one thing, and I shall believe you.'

The interior qualities come to the fore, asserting themselves over the physical. In contrast to skin, hair, shining eye and firm flesh, the following tend to be foremost: intelligence, generosity, dignity, listening to others, a capacity for understanding.

But there must be *something inside to come to the fore*: physical decay will be compensated for by the brilliance within. It will not be necessary to mutilate oneself with unreasonable surgery, excessive make-up, flamboyant dress – or skulk because we are mature, or we are already old.

If the transformation effected in our body is inexorable, its speed and character depend on genes, care, health, interior vitality as well. With the inexorable there is only one way out, and it will not be by running away: it is by living with the inexorable the best way I can. The issue is not that life should be suspended, but that we move with it, instead of paralysing ourselves and hanging back.

If we were not too foolish, we should revel in our appearance at all stages. Look in the mirror and say, 'Good, that is me.' Not extraordinarily preserved, nor excessively destroyed. I am how one is at this phase. And if I am like this, I like me.

I am my history.

If we are not merely our appearance, *we are also our appearance*. To deny that is in effect to deny what we have become. It is, therefore, sad to neglect appearance, pathetic if we want to look 20 at the age of 40, or look 40 at 70. We should want to be beautiful, dignified, elegant and vital beings – from the ages of 60 to 80.

Still happy at 80.

~

I was lent a book where the phrase was underlined: *the goal of all life is death.*

However, I believe that *the end of life is death*, but that *the goal of life is a happy life.*

Words wear out like stones in a river: they change their shape and meaning, their place; some disappear, become mud in the bed of the waters. They reappear later, renewed.

Happiness is one such word.

It has become commonplace because we live in an age of vulgarisation of great emotions and desires, everything – fast food, ready-to-wear, microwave-ready – is quick and easy, and so often anaemic.

If by enchantment and occupation I chose the territory of words, I know how some are corrupted by use and become aggressive or contradictory, take on airs of irony or ingenuity. They become confused and ineffective, lend themselves to misunderstandings or their connotation is muddied.

I know a little of how they grasp our experiences and give them countenances, clothes, airs that we had not imagined.

I like startling elements – in persons and words. But some words and circumstances shock me when I peer behind their seven veils. Many are decked in the transformations of our time, in the patterns of behaviour, progress and advance, but also in dark and sterile anxiety, waste. Some have to do with ideals that not only do we rarely achieve, but even when we do have little to do with freedom and happiness.

The passage of time means I become more and more complete, if I do not drag with me the basic preconception of our era: that only youth is beautiful and has the right to be happy, that maturity is destitute of charm and old age is a curse.

Taming to avoid being devoured

The age of maturity does not need to be the beginning of the end; an advanced age need not mean isolation and safety. Both can strengthen loving ties, family links, friendship, changing interests, greater enjoyment of good things.

To exist is to be able to refine our awareness that we are too precious to waste ourselves in trying to be something we are not, cannot be, and do not wish to be.

~

'Time is like that: it devours everything by the edges, by gnawing, nibbling, cutting and eating. And nothing and nobody will escape, except by making it his pet creature.'[1]

The reader accompanying me in this book will help me to unwind the time reflected, the time thought, the time hated and feared, the time conquered.

Why are we so afraid of time?

Why and when do we decide that it will always be a threat and not a promise? Or when were we taught to think in this way, and why do we accept it?

We live in a civilisation that has granted us more time but detests the passage of time.

'You assert that time does not exist; so why write so much about it?' the journalist asks.

She is – and is not – right. Time has been the backcloth or even a character in my writings. By asserting it does not exist I

[1] Lya Luft, *O Ponto Cego*, Sao Paulo: Record, 2003

mean that it does not exist as something determining my beliefs or pessimism, *if I do not want this*. It is not a powerful external entity that from a certain age (defined arbitrarily or by world health organisations) drives me downhill without my being able to react.

People can react in many positive ways: by taking on and valuing every phase of themselves; not resigning to the general judgement, nor giving up as soon as the wrinkles appear; never falling into the false rebellion that transforms us into a caricature of youth.

Some prevailing concepts about the possible joys of maturity are pathetic. A woman of 65 on her own bought a new apartment. The comments she received were encouraging, but some left her disconcerted:

'With this beautiful apartment, you must have heaps of men.'

'Near your new block a modern gym has opened. Surely you'll have no difficulty meeting toy boys now.'

In this contemptible kingdom of futility, these concepts do not encourage life, but a freeze-up. They do not suggest the construction of positive values, but the sowing of ground with stupidities. Time will be the ogre who eats small children, and the crisis moments are going to bounce us from one side to the other, like rag dolls, human beings stuffed with straw.

If my gaze gives meaning to the real, and to the exterior, I can declare that the world has room for me regardless of my physical beauty or appearance or age. But if my gaze sees everything through lenses of the most stupid or cynical superficiality, I must pack my bags and retire before, well before, the fullness of maturity.

Like so many other things, life will change my body. Over my soul it will have only the power I grant it.

Only if we permit it will this most intimate companion of ours – the time in which we travel – become our executioner. We shall spend our existence bound to a scarecrow that instead of chasing away harmful birds inhibits our own potential for flying.

The trick is to invert the game.

Accept as natural what is natural; accept gracefully what cannot be changed. There are so many good reasons to live well, and exciting things to discover, which earlier I might not have had the opportunity or knowledge even to try.

~

We are so frivolous that we make ourselves incapable of loving life as it is given to us and conquering its difficulties at every stage. We are dominated by an anxiety that is not a positive impulse that leads us to produce, to be open to new possibilities, but the childish agitation of someone who is never content because he never finds herself. What ensues is fragmentation and loss.

If we are outside the norms – conventions determined by others (not always real, not always very respectable) – by being too big or very fat or very old or less polished or less rich or less powerful, we do not allow ourselves to be naturally desirable and loving.

So we do not let ourselves be loved.

A mature or old body can be healthy and harmonious just as a young body can be diseased or misshapen. *But for us to compare a mature or old body to a body in the fullness of its freshness is childish and cruel.*

To have more tranquillity, more knowledge and to strengthen one's own ideas – in sum, to be an individual – demands reflection, firmness and individuality. But such ideas are obsolete, out of fashion. We are constantly called upon to *enjoy life* – whatever that may mean.

When I was a young girl I would hear (and sometimes I still hear) such things as: 'Don't marry young – you must first enjoy yourself!' This was meaningful only for the boys: the girls were preparing to be submissive and gentle. Today I hear: 'Don't think of having children early – enjoyment must come first!'

I could not say what I think of the expression, because I do not use it. What I know is that *enjoying* has nothing essentially to do with acquiring, buying, taking pleasure, possessing, travelling, dancing, love-making, consuming. All this is a part, and is fine, but what exactly is this *enjoyment*?

For some, it is always being in fashion, even though the model on offer is totally beyond (or outside) our wildest dreams. For others, it is to have consumer goods well beyond their own needs.

Tethered like defenceless animals to ideas that we do not even approve of, we are victims of fantasies created and sustained by the media, by industry, by fashion, by commerce – who want to sell us this iconic merchandise, valued above everything: *beauty of the moment, and eternal youth.*

The horror of physical difference is so widespread that it is quite common when asking after someone, to hear the response (accompanied by a meaningful gesture):

'How's your daughter?'

'She's too fat!'

'And how is so-and-so?'

'Well, that one's huge!'

It does not occur to them that I might want to know if the person is travelling, has had another child, has finished studying, is ill or happy, has retired, has remarried.

Our current obsession, even before money and social status, is with physical appearance. So living is not about making progress, but consuming and losing weight. Notwithstanding that it is a part of growing that in my childhood my bones lengthened, and my shoe size is no longer 7.5. It is a part of growing that in maturity the body should change and further transformations ensue.

It is part of the process of life, not of death, that at 60, 70, 80 my pace should be less agile, my skin wrinkled, my body less upright, my eyes less shining. But it is *not* part of that process that I should regard myself as disposable and skulk in the shadows without the right to move about, act, participate actively – within my natural limitations.

'I have not been to the swimming pool for years; you don't imagine I'm going to let anyone see my body in the state it's in!'

By trying to be what one was 20 or 40 years ago, anyone with this kind of talk will feel he no longer exists; will think that the person in the mirror is not a continuation of the previous person, but a freak of nature.

~

Losses and Gains

Regardless of genes, real potential, age, we are always frustrated because we are not more blond, more brunette, thinner, taller, more athletic, smoother-skinned or do not have more seductive eyes.

Why do we accept and cultivate the pathetic idea that only youth is good and beautiful, with the right to dare, to renew, to love? With the right to be, to have scope?

Sufferings (I am speaking of the avoidable) come in good measure from the fact that we are so childish. Beyond grief for what we are not physically, we suffer for what we still have to do:

Buy all the products.

Visit all the fashionable places.

Above all: never relax, never be content, never accept ourselves.

To stop to think, or not to think, would be too grievous.

This is not the sign of an unquiet mind, but of a precarious soul. This is not living a life, much less enjoying it.

In the same way there is no abrupt halt in the midst of this race for the sudden awareness that one exists as a complex human being, with a path and destiny.

We do not on a sudden whim invoke the moment to love, the moment to be decent, generous, reflective, looking within the self and within those who live with me. The moment to question myself. The moment to show the children something of what I am thinking, the moment to be, with my love, a companion and faithful accomplice.

We do not function like that.

Our phases are not divided up by dykes and bulwarks: they are a current of running water. However, it must be natural, must be part of the living together, not an instant thrust into the routine – like a foreign body – when we are anxious or guilty. The love that engages in dialogue is a habit. If it is never practised, it cannot be expected to yield good, ripe fruit.

Even in sexuality, despite ostentation, liberation and the incredible multiplicity of messages (most fairly questionable), we remain very basic.

We end up surrendering to the obligation to be sexual phenomena (almost always a lie and trick from insecurity), but as human beings we are probably uncertain. If the media offer me ten modestly priced lessons on how to be happy in bed – or out of it – it might be as well to analyse and conclude that this is a decoy, that *happiness in loving does not come from performance, but from tenderness that brings to the fore and intensifies the performance.*

We must learn to struggle against absurd models; to discover who I am, what I like, how I like to be – how I can be happier. This is not in the magazines, on television, in the comments of friends: it is intimate, personal, non-transferable. Each of us needs to understand and construct it.

Happiness is like that: each person, each day, accepts what the market offers – or makes his own decisions.

4

Losing without losing the self

Flown are the loves I had
or that had me:
they have gone
in a silent and shining procession.
Time has taught me
not to believe too much in death
nor to give up on life: I cultivate
joys in a garden
where we are I, past dreams,
old loves and their secrets.
It is hope – that shines forth
like pebbles of colour between the roots.[1]

My lover, Hope

In the prime of youth she tried to kill herself. On waking in the
hospital she came upon a nurse who asked her: 'But why, why?'

Lya Luft, *Secreta Mirada*, Sao Paulo: Ediciones Siciliano e Mandarim, 1997

She answered, succinctly, clearly, full of her own pain: 'No hope.'

~

We all know those days with no horizon in view. Experience teaches us that they pass, unless we are sick or we are inveterate pessimists by nature or conditioning.

To be more or less an optimist depends on upbringing, family environment, genetic predisposition (ah, the genetics of the soul . . .), passing situations. Obviously it is easy to be confident when one is content.

But we are not only our circumstances, we are also our essence.

The great pessimist collects all the disaster stories in the newspaper and sends them to his friends every morning, believes that the human being is worthless, the world a mere platform for wars and corruption. The excessive optimist believes reality is one of television soaps and adolescent dreams, fashions, magazines, beaches, clubs. The sensible person (not the graceless, not the tiresome) knows that the human being is no great thing, but likes it; that life is a struggle, but wants to live it well; that there exist – as well as injustice, betrayal and suffering – beauty and affection and moments of splendour. That you can trust without being betrayed at any moment by someone who loves you.

I may be an essential pessimist, by nature or conditioning or circumstances. However, I may only be depressed.

To emerge from a phase of depression there are a thousand resources available to anyone. Therapy, a good walk, a new love, dyeing the hair, dinner in a delightful place, changing the position of the garden urns, seeing what is happening in the arts. Reading, reflection, observing within and without. Buying a dog, going to football, planning a journey (could even be just across the way). Trying to be in touch with art, whatever it may be. Taking new interests and finding affection, cultivating them.

But if I embrace my depression or my black vision of everything, if I thereby expect a cry for the attention of others, to punish them (or myself), I may therefore be opting for eternal discontent. Gradually I shall be ousted from the circle of those who are the vital lovers of hope.

~

Even after the years have ravaged much (perhaps the family, work, my body, my loves), what was good can remain – not shadows or void, but reason to return and flourish. Dragging the chair out of the shady area and seating myself in the sun for a while. After the first horror of some grave loss has passed, in the darkness of impotence and discordance, loopholes begin to open through which the former clarity peeps through to the present.

This table in this room, this child and that friend, this sound on the piano, the tree branch people tried to cut, the hillside where one walked many years before – everything summons us: no longer to weep for the past, but to project into the present what was beautiful and is not lost.

And people become aware of what they also owe to the loves they had, the friends they had almost forgotten, the house that was sold along with part of childhood, the person they were through all these years. Life can be good again: with someone else or alone, in another house, with other friends, with new possessions or among the old ones.

A light always comes from beautiful things that are past, as does an ability to see the most commonplace with some enchantment. This is the *wonderful secret* that all can enjoy but which is muddied by haste, by an overload of chores and the demand that we be what we cannot be.

To live any phase with joy, to live with elegance and vitality, it is essential to believe that it is worthwhile. That there are ways of being happy, happier, and we can pursue them. But this is not a chase for treasures bought with money: it is an interior pursuit, of our values, our value, our beliefs and our genuine desire.

Do I want, do I need to have this body, this sexuality, these consumer goods that others expect of me – or am I more content as I am, savouring what I can acquire and planning what I can transform?

To decide this we must open scope for recollection, observation and self-observation within our routine. What is required is *the active silence of someone thinking*.

But it is difficult to escape social convention that on the one hand brings a vast collection of books and courses that speak of meditation, reflection, spirituality (which is itself becoming fashionable), and on the other hand directs by all means that *people do something*: must travel, be active, go out, be seen.

One must be joyful and busy, must be seen, know the fashionable spots, be chic, travel – not so much to broaden the horizons, as to be able to join in discussions with friends or acquaintances later on the newest restaurant, the most modern gallery, the most outlandish store.

One must be happy at a determined time, at weekends, just as some couples must make love (exclusively) on Saturday afternoons.

Losing without losing the self

~

In youth we are apprentices, we are amateurs in life. In maturity we must be good professionals of living: clear-sighted and still optimists, more serene, with a different beauty, productive and efficient.

But I am told that after a certain phase I can no longer change direction, house, clothes, place. Even in the worst relationship I should not think of separating, not fall in love (even though I am free), not have a good sex life (even though I am healthy).

Shall we have no choice, if we pass a 'certain age'? With the passage of time does 'our time' really pass?

The choice is ours, individually. We have a choice, but we are insecure. We can change, but we do not believe this. Much of this hesitation comes from outside, from the comments of others, from superficial propositions, from foolish models.

'To live and be happy should not be so complicated,' someone complained. Is it because people do not at least simplify what could be uncomplicated?

Maturing should be refinement in the search for simplicity.

I write in my novels about our dark side, about conflict and drama. I try to unveil the dark visage, of perversity, self-destruction, the accumulation of rage and resentment to be found in the human being. But I do not believe it is mainly so. I enjoy people. I am in solidarity with the fictional characters I created with my imagination.

Anyone who does not know me and thinks of me from my books as a remote or sombre being is mistaken: an incorrigible optimist lives in me who believes in being happy; in renewal, in overcoming, in survival – not as a remnant and wreck, but as a complete being at every stage.

I believe that living is doing and creating: the fatalities of disease and death are inevitable. The rest – the whole vast interior and exterior – I myself construct. I am the mistress of my destiny. But it is more convenient to complain about fate instead of reviewing my choices and improving my plans.

'How can I be an optimist, if my mother suffers from Alzheimer's and my husband has retired on little money and is at home depressed, my son has not found his path; if my hands are blotched, my neck wrinkled, my breasts more fallen?'

People manage.

Not necessarily with new sexual techniques, not with brand-name goods, not in the fashionable club or on the smartest beach: it is here that I learn this. In the silence of my home, my body, my thought. In the strength of my decision, perhaps in my vaulting transgression.

If I accept the idea that everything closes when youth comes to an end, the possibility of my being someone authentic decreases each year. This prospect induces inertia and squandering of talents that might be nurtured to the end, without age mattering.

When, after separation from the father of my children, I remade my life with someone else, the expression I heard most often from friends was: 'But at your age should people still try to be happy again?'

I was astounded: 'Friend, I am only 46, not 146!'

This sharpened my interest in the matter: we are modern and so ancient; we are liberated and so limited; we are of a new millennium and we do not, at least *with intelligence*, accept the passage of time and our passage in time.

Losing without losing the self

When youth passes, we begin at last to grow. We learn to relax, to have more humour, to run more skilfully with negative factors, to pay more heed to what is happening around us. Happiness demands patience: it is addition, increase, conquest and perfection.

~

At a talk on new interests in maturity and old age I noted that 90 per cent of the audience were women.

I asked a doctor colleague at the speakers' table: 'Where are the men who should be at this gathering?'

He teasingly returned the question: 'When did you last hear of outings for widowers or talks for men?'

I had never thought of this. Why do they not exist? Is it because there are fewer widowers, since they die before the wives, and those who are on their own rarely remain on their own, as they soon go and look for another helpmate? It is possible.

Is it because many of them, on their own, give up, then become depressed, or rely more on their children? Likewise.

Is it because they are more taken up with their work if they do not take needless early retirement? The same.

They will be less inhibited by the idea imposed on them that there can be no change, that it is essential to conquer and to hold on to a position, that going backwards is feeble.

In addition, women have a greater capacity to form ties, to nurture affection, to meet as a group. They show more solidarity and more support for each other. Perhaps because they have a greater propensity for joy.

I see women travelling on their own, or in pairs or groups, enjoying themselves, learning about places and things, cultivating interests, engaging in new relationships, returning to study. Interacting and progressing.

I do not so often see men doing the same. I am not conscious of their travelling as a pair or in groups. Returning to study, rarely. Why not be a post-graduate at 70, for example? Or go to a public library for the first time to see what there is in the books? What is new to see in the cinemas?

Whatever it is, we all need to find a solution for the inhibiting fear of the passage of time, which is after all fear of living. We prefer not to live so that we do not waste our soul, confined within the shell of alienation.

But how can one have determination when it seems something is lost every day?

Something is lost.

Much is lost.

I have today a short list of people whom I loved who moved away or died; if I should live to be 80 the list will certainly have grown. But I have a charming list of people who have arrived: not only grandchildren, but new friends of all ages. Not to mention technical innovations I want to know or use, the discoveries I shall try to follow, the books to read, the things to do.

The other day I asked my doctor daughter if I might not be dehydrated, since my skin was different. She looked, smiled with that maternal quirkiness our daughters sometimes display to us, and said with affectionate charm, 'Mother, you are 60, aren't you? That's all it is.'

We laughed together, in the typical complicity of mothers and daughters.

Losing without losing the self

Not for a second was I nostalgic for the skin I had when I was 20, because it was accompanied by all the afflictions (and delights) of that stage, from which I am spared today.

I took a good look in the mirror with the glasses that I have always needed for reading. True: much has changed. I am not finished, but different from what I was. Physically I am different from the girl and the young woman.

What am I going to do? Despair, be ashamed, want to go backwards? I prefer to be amused, face things with the realistic sense that I have changed, and with the knowledge that those who love me go on loving me in spite of everything – or because of everything.

'But how is it possible for something to improve with age?' I am asked with vague indignation.

I began to tot up, half in fun: to begin with, I enjoy myself much more at work. Writing, publishing, waiting for the reviews and sales of my first novel at 40 was ecstatic and scary. Today, with so many books published and so many faithful readers, I really do not worry in the least. I no longer need to prove myself; I need only to do what I do with a lighter hand (never less seriousness), more joy. More demands, that is so, but without undue tension.

It never occurred to me to be aggressive with regard to my colleagues, since I soon learned that in our field of work there is room for many, for all. I can rejoice at the success of others without fearing that it affects my own small achievement.

Is it because I am generous?

No: it is because although I am often muddled, mistaken, often commit all conceivable futilities, I do not have the panic or insecurity of when I was aged 20. Nor that endearing touch of arrogance that makes the young think the world is ours – and must render us homage.

My body is changing as it has been since I was born. My heart is transformed by every experience. It still beats, jumps and is frightened. I am still vulnerable to the beautiful and good, to disaster and disappointment, just as when I was aged 10.

This is what we are: this mixture, this contradiction, this continual questioning. We are alive.

Also I do not seek to assert that maturity is 'better' than youth, old age 'better' than maturity: I say that every moment is *my* moment, and I must try to live it in the best way possible, with realism, with sensibility, with a grain of audacity, and with all possible joy.

Inside I am still the small girl who is frightened or amused by some foolishness the others do not understand, busy as they are with more important matters. I divide myself between daydream and practical life, without properly knowing to which I belong. With time I understood that this indefiniteness is only apparent, that the ambiguity has made me strong. I conjured up many things in my novels; I learned that good humour can help love.

It has some advantages, this 'end of autumn' of which the poet Carlos Drummond de Andrade speaks.

What freedom it is to no longer have to decide on professional paths and assert myself in them, beget and rear children, buy houses, cope with budgets, fear the immensity of the future – and whether there will be a place for me in it.

Many a matter that was in its time dramatic is today a memory that makes me smile sympathetically about something that unfolded from such a mess.

If someone loves me now, it will not be for a beautiful body that inevitably must change, but for what I am undisguisedly today. No splendid young woman of 20 threatens me: I am on another plane.

I had losses, and they multiplied with the passage of time. I had gains, in a balance that does not make me feel treated unjustly. In particular, I never lost the stubborn confidence that drives me to carry on when the first step seems too difficult.

~

If we are open to renewal and change we are alive, whatever stage we are at. And if a new love appears we can at any moment be reborn for that. We no longer need to bear children, establish a family (I did want this greatly and it brought me immense joy).

We fulfil many duties. We make mistakes, because that is necessary too. We suffer, because this is part of it.

The children who were tied to our skirt are today's adults, close to us or remote, but our offspring still. The maternal bond has enriched itself and changed. We may even share a little with them when we are living out some story.

'But what story?'

'Heaven knows, a new plan, a journey, a course, a friendship, a love affair.'

'Love affair? At this time?'

Mothers and grandmothers, fathers and grandfathers are active, travelling, loving, studying, and simply being sapient and capable human beings to a fairly advanced age. But in some families, woe betide divorcees or widows who think of embarking on a new love affair.

They are the inconsistencies of a culture that evolved randomly: seems modern, but continues to be ancient and immature.

'I can't take a lover, my children will kill me! Introduce my lover at home? Unthinkable, my children will think me laughable!'

It will depend on each of us whether our life is our own territory or merely begrudgingly on loan from others – even the children. It may be the field for running in pursuit of plans and gathering shared experiences, or a narrow pit where we hide and await the final blow.

～

'The time that gnaws and corrodes must be restored,' said a character of mine, and I add: 'to our benefit'.

We waste a lot of time trying to fool time. We mature inexorably but we do not feel more serene, or more content.

'How can I feel content at this instant, at the age of 50? At 60 worse, at 70 disaster!'

There are many fine things we can do in maturity, which we did not accomplish in youth. Availability, experience, freedom and vision were lacking. We were too busy, too tense, too fragmented.

If there is nothing urgent to 'do', then generally we take this as a cue to act, agitate, run, invent something. It could be simple contemplation. Thinking. Reading. Gazing. Walking.

When we least expect it, something specific pops up before us to 'do'.

Instead of indulging the empty nest syndrome (given that

offspring remain our offspring even if they no longer live with us), we could fill this void with a thousand things to do. We could discover, perhaps, that we can expand and grow more freely without so many demands within the home. Those demands were good, they were joyful, they were even exciting and tricky, but the time is different now.

It cannot be construed as no time, however: and this makes a big difference.

~

Rethinking and reshaping themselves personally made many women come out of the shadows in maturity to assert themselves in work, science and art. When the children grew up, when monotony was creeping in, they discovered abundant energy and vitality: unexplored paths lay open before them. They went out to uncover them.

Many women did not wake up. Many were in a rut. Many lost direction. One or more felt that giving up was preferable to venturing out. But a good proportion took wing and produced, and took part – and still flourished.

In my case insecurity or accommodation had decreed that I should not write except for my columns and poems. The game that had so much appealed to me from childhood, of writing fiction, seemed forbidden: self-confidence was lacking. The audacity, that for some people comes only in maturity or even later, was lacking.

I adopted the comfortable position 'Me? Just imagine!' that exonerates us from serious risk. I had an intuition that in writing novels I would draw from within me dramatic characters, evoke fears and doubts well beyond my personal experience – since we speak for others, for many, for all. What strange creatures would burst open the cupboards where they were locked up – and what would they do with me?

What scope would they demand in my organised routine?

Why drag from their repose disquiets that were so carefully filed away?

The fateful 'opinion of others' still constrained me a little: writing and publishing was one of the final exorcisms of this devil that was never particularly active in me, but was lurking there in his corner.

At the age of 40 I wrote my first novel: until then I did not really know my value from a professional perspective. At home the recurrent dialogue came:

'I cannot find what use I am from a professional perspective.'

'So why not dedicate yourself more to your literature?'

'But how would I do that?'

'You will find out.'

I found out. With pain and difficulty, I ended up finding the path. And I observed that at that moment in our culture many women were beginning to grow as human beings and as professionals, at more or less at my age, and with similar experiences to me.

I perceived when probably halfway through my life span that I still had much to do. Like so many women, I saw it was not the moment to think of stopping, to fear the menopause, the children leaving home, the future or to mourn the passing of youth, but to restructure, develop, even to begin much that was new.

Maturing began there. It was a sequence of discoveries, with much difficulty and much joy.

Someone who loved me encouraged me through his confidence in me. I shall always be grateful to him for this: for the love that, instead of capturing and controlling me, freed me and helped me to grow.

~

One of the questions – perhaps the fundamental question – is what and how much do we allow ourselves. The tendency is to allow ourselves little, and to follow the current: at this moment in time? in your situation? but do you really believe that . . . ?

My friend divorced, and being on her own she bought a huge bright apartment, where a whole family could be housed comfortably.

Instead of applauding her, encouraging her, many people were astonished: 'Why are you on your own in so big an apartment?'

Why, on her own, should she be accommodated in a small place – as if she no longer deserved space? It is how women talk when their children have gone and perhaps the husband has died: 'Is she mad, living alone in that mansion?'

But why (except for genuine questions of security, for example) should she not continue dwelling in a big house, to entertain children, grandchildren and friends, and hold parties – or simply because she enjoys it?

The interior space is necessary for the continual recreation of self. Accommodation should be on the brightest and most generous scale. There we can analyse the course we have run, establish new boundaries, rethink past loves and future plans.

Nonetheless in this culture of ours of noise and agitation we are impelled to *do* things, promote things, not to reflect on them: we need events, itineraries and programmes, or we feel left outside and behind.

However, what truly reinvigorates us is relaxation, self-examination, reflection. Nothing renews, innovates, expands and becomes true without a moment of silence and observation. Then we can, must, aspire and venture.

We are not saved by a mediocre and bureaucratic archive of the soul, but by a bold sweep within the self to find the essential material, and to take off with this, sometimes without even a safety net or certainty.

It is not necessary to be out a great deal to share in the miracle and eventual upheavals of living. People can have a full, conscious, worthy existence even within the quiet of their living room or at their work table.

Thanks to the myth of a writer who still writes in longhand and detests innovations, journalists have asked me more than once what I think of the Internet, the World Wide Web, the computer, the mobile phone, technology and scientific advances.

Going by air is better than going by carriage; to communicate by e-mail with a loved person several times day – and having conditions to do this – is better than writing a fortnightly letter. Protecting a child with a vaccine is better than leaving her exposed to smallpox, mumps, measles and hepatitis.

Although it is a matter of taste and custom, using a pen can have its appeal, but it is many years since I thought of writing and translating in longhand: the computer is the gentle and highly efficient servant that facilitates my work.

It makes no sense to opt to remain more isolated when so many things are on offer at my door, on my television, on my computer – unless I would prefer to curl up in my tiny interior room without windows and perhaps without a door.

Some people like to shut themselves up in a cavern.

It is a matter of choice, and you can make it. But, please, do not freeze the atmosphere around you with the vapours of your frozen soul.

To sum up: first, progress is here to stay. Swimming against the rapids is a useless discomfort at the least, and can seem arrogant or stupid. Second, it is better to look at things from a positive perspective. We have never had so much communication: friends who never exchanged letters (letters are obsolete, aren't they?), 'talk' on a daily basis by e-mail. Those who might be in bitter solitude make new friends through chat rooms. Lovers apart can cultivate a new kind of 'presence'. The universe is at our disposal: the most recent genetic discoveries, books that we had not yet heard about. I can visit the great museums, read about every work, take a close look at every detail. I can know distant cities, listen to music, play chess. The choice is almost infinite. The trash and the treasure of cultures are there for me.

'And what do you think of dating or even having sex on the Internet?'

How childish we are, how childish some of our interrogations are. Endearing for all that. I answer that there is nothing more original than what was done or is done by the people of other times or of our time with specialist magazines.

Losses and Gains

We attach too much importance to all these preconceptions, details, prurience, censorship, when there is so much to shine forth. In the wide sea of the wide world, where technologies are not good or bad: it depends on how they are used.

The gregarious will use the computer to contact people, research, open up to the whole universe. The depressive will seek to isolate himself further. The neurotic will exercise his great or small manias.

~

Finally, after so many wanderings we seem to mature – from the chronological point of view at least.

We seem to arrive at a comfortable landing. We overcome grief, we accomplish tasks; already we are achieving things that seemed unthinkable in youth.

Now is the time to lean back and delineate plans for freedom: a journey, a new course, books to read, grief to forget, friends to meet. Do something with my plants. Open the blinds and be thrilled because the morning is dazzling and we have an hour to walk in streets we have frequented for many years: every leaf, every wall is an intimate acquaintance – and that is also good.

But the old bothersome, cunning little goblin spots us and sticks its tongue out. And now, and now? Is it going to be just this, this haven?

We fear, perhaps, that from here on everything will be encapsulated in this interior comfort where memories nest, everything is disentangled and resolved . . . we think.

The task of living never ends, unless people so decide.

Losing without losing the self

Dream and astonishment breathe in our ears when everything appears dormant. Soon the certainty of having at last arrived at an immutable point of accommodation will begin to waver.

Something new is positioned next to the armchair where perhaps we were innocently watching television. A word heard, a phrase read, a new countenance, an old acquaintance, a trifle stirs us. We emerge from the agreeable torpor, we poke our head out of the cocoon for a better view.

We can choose:

I shall stay asleep.

I am going to the next corner to see what is going on.

This moment defines the continuation of an existence in motion or crystallised, tuned or out of tune.

This potential for choice startles us but it is only a sign that we have embarked, we are in motion and in transformation.

Even now that baggage of our innate tendencies, outside influence and past experiences will determine how the next years will be. And, pay attention: this happens at any instant – if we are not yet made of straw.

'What's up with you?' friends ask.

'You seem so well!' colleagues say.

'I heard you singing in the bath!' the children remark.

Gradually this new breath of air, which could be a plan, work, travel, new friendship or love affair, will come into focus. Its voice is clear and calls our name.

Perhaps people do not yet understand, but fate – that lays good ambushes and disasters where we fall drastically because we are alive – smiles nodding with our new lover: *life*.

The future lies in our hands once more.

Letter to a friend who has no e-mail

You will think me half mad and interfering with this letter, which will be long. I shall have to send it by courier (a good thing that it does not have to be by a messenger on horse between two distant castles . . .) instead of sending it to you immediately as an e-mail attachment, since you, although you could, still refuse to have a computer, detest every kind of modernism, and think that *your time has passed*.

I dreamed about you last night, on your own and desolate in an enormous empty house on barren ground. Then, in the same house, now surrounded by trees and flowers, you were organising a renovation: hammer-blows, people preparing delicious food, friends gathering for a party. You had told me that you would never allow any renovation in your house; everything should remain as it was 30 years ago. Whoever heard of never renewing anything in the house, or in people?

I thought the dream so symbolic that I decided to tell you about it.

You are a good man, educated, refined, depressed and resigned. Some scraps of good humour even in the depression show that you will snap out of it – if you wish.

I am going to give you some ideas that you will regard as peevish, but I ask you to think about them. They do not come from a silly little girl and they do come from a woman who has already been in the kingdom of shadows and returned.

Do not be sorry for yourself. You are not the victim of anything. You said that you were in shock on realising that you had 'missed the bus because you were not ready, had not heeded the signals'. So give up this remoteness, take the plunge, surrender. If necessary, take the fateful leap: it might be a last chance.

Changing is difficult, daring still more. I know. There were times when I woke up thinking: I might live another 20, 30 years in the situation I am now in. Do I want to go on as I am?

A new interior attitude at least would depend entirely on me and the rest would accrue. I did not always achieve it. I was not always on target. However, stirring oneself is better than staying in the quicksand where the longer we remain the more we become trapped.

In general, the practical things we can do to innovate are simple.

They depend on an interior attitude allied to concrete possibilities such as money and taste. For a housewife, cleaning out cupboards, chucking out some of the useless old stuff, or rearranging the furniture to her taste – even if others in the house complain – can be a start. To you, I would say, for example (intentionally running the risk of seeming incredibly futile to you): buy a computer. Go on the Internet to research, discover or entertain and inform yourself. Stay switched on.

Choose the positive in modernity. Why stop outside with a hangdog look? There are really beautiful things to be savoured. Innovations are not disasters for being new, but are daughters of progress, marvels of our technology, interesting tools, motivation to become more whole and more participatory.

Get to know some of the places you say you hate for being 'in fashion'. I am not suggesting that you go to a nightclub, but to one of those agreeable places, new, where one eats well and sees interesting people. Cloistering yourself is no help to anyone, much less to you.

Do not boycott air conditioning by suffering heat only because you think 'air conditioning is ruinous to health'. If it were so, half the population of Europe and the United States, where heating is ubiquitous, would be dead.

I know professionals in your field, old, very old, who are still active or just keep themselves up-to-date and are active for pure pleasure. Perhaps you could make a come-back? It is not true that a profession 'drops people'. It is always the people who remain in the air, unheeding. Sometimes this is recoverable.

Plan a good journey. Use your time and money (since you have enough at least) for your enjoyment. Life is a laid table: it has mortal poisons and delicious dishes that bring pleasure. There are some who choose the poison, and those who grab the delights. I hope that you do not believe that pleasure is impossible or a disaster.

Choose the positive. *Desire to be a little happy*, be enthusiastic for something within your circumstances – but outside your pessimism.

Or, if none of this is possible because this is *your way* and your option, at least do not think ill of me for this letter that was, if not a hello, perhaps an error of . . . *my way*.

Old age, why not?

For Granny, beauty was a torment, because time did not stay still and since she was a small girl her greatest fear was to lose that supreme gift. She would look in the mirror peering for the first wrinkle, a first fold. A first blotch.

Losing without losing the self

When she reached the age of 60 she almost died of grief, went about the house crying out: 'I hate being 60! I can't stand being 60!'

It was no good people saying that she did not even look 40, so well preserved was she. They pleaded with her: 'Try to imagine that you are conquering maturity instead of losing youth; and that one day you will gain old age instead of losing maturity. Isn't it much more natural to think like this?'

But Granny would not accept; for her the natural was not natural: 'I hate to think I'm growing old. I don't accept, don't accept, finishing.'

The first minor surgeries had done her good: they removed a bitter trace, a sign of premature weariness. Then her doctor told her: 'Let's leave nature to work for a while and the body to rest. Don't abuse it.'

So then she went to look for other doctors, who would follow her wishes. Challenging the unchallengeable and exceeding its boundaries, she was entering the unreal.

But the illusions did not stay the time any more, and the stitching began to unstitch. My grandmother was isolating herself. She gave up her friendships, stopped the parties, no longer liked anyone. She began to delude herself, claiming that everybody was pointing at her in the streets, in shops, in restaurants. There goes that old woman.

Increasingly more difficult to deal with and to live with, she demanded what nobody could give her: a freeze on time. Little by little she was being devoured from within as well.

The countenance of my grandmother, from being mended so much, became another's. She changed the eye, changed the nose, changed the chin, even changed the ear. In the end nothing was hers.[1]

[1]Lya Luft, *O Ponto Cego*, Sao Paulo: Record, 2003

~

If we want to freeze time and isolate ourselves in this cocoon, we shall be liquidated even before youth is over. We shall be our fiction. Reality goes on around us, and one day we shall discover that we are outside it.

For some this will be the saving crisis. The invention of a phantasmal 'us' has ended.

If we still want to live, not vegetate on the shelf of our fantasy, we must find in this affliction what has remained of our personality. For this is what will give us coherence and capacity to grow to the last beam of clarity.

Thus one can have control, not over time, but over the extent to which it will favour or destroy us.

To understand that maturity and old age are not decline but transformation, we must be prepared. Ready to face *existence as a whole*, with various stages, varied forms of beauty and even of happiness. To believe that with care and luck we can be active even decades later: this must be conquered inch by inch.

However, even in childhood we were warned that soon something bad was in store for us:

'When you reach my age, you'll see,' mothers, aunts, grandmothers would say.

'Enjoy being a child; when you grow up the party will be over!' they would advise with a touch of spite.

'I'm very old for this kind of thing,' they would protest at a moment of fun and joy.

Existing in time was presented to us as an ill-omened race: every day a loss, every year a holding back. Who did not have moments of wanting never to grow up to escape these vague threats?

Being contradictory – and thereby interesting – it is no wonder that in the era in which we are most alive there is so much flight from what is conventionally called *old age*. Since we imagine that our final decades are merely decline, we strengthen the taboo inherent in these words.

Words mean emotions and concepts, hence preconceptions. So I want to talk of my implacability with the implacability we have with the terms – and the reality – *old person, old age.*

We detest or we fear old age for its brand of incapacity and isolation. It is something to be avoided like a disease. It is nothing but foolish to look upon time as a series of separate drawers in which we are young, mature or old – allowing only one of them – that of youth – the right to joys and achievements, since the possibility of having health, plans and tenderness to the age of 90 is real, within the limitations of each stage.

When we can no longer carry on business, travel to distant countries or take walks, we can still read, listen to music, gaze upon nature, show affection, gather people to our side, observe those around us, eventually give them shelter and a shoulder.

For this it is unnecessary to be young, beautiful (meaning firm flesh and silky skin) or agile, but we must still be *clear-sighted*. To have acquired a relative wisdom and a sensible optimism – things that can improve with the passage of years. But the idea prevails that old age is a sentence from which one must flee at all costs – to the extent even of mutilating or hiding ourselves. In the spirit of the herd that characterises us, we adopt this hypothesis, without much discussion, although it is to our disadvantage. This is manifest in the haste with which we add, as an excuse: 'Yes, you are and I am old at 80 but . . . we are young in spirit.'

Why should being young in spirit be better than having a mature or old spirit?

Having greater wisdom, serenity, elegance before facts that in youth would make us tear our hair out, does not seem to me totally undesirable. I am going to hate it if, when I am old, someone wants to praise me by saying that I am young in spirit.

I think the mature spirit much more interesting than the young. More serene, more mysterious, more seductive.

Similarly I did not like it when a critic, thinking to please me, once wrote that although I was a woman I wrote 'with a man's hand'. In order to be good the literature composed by a woman does not need to rely on the assessment 'but she writes like a man'.

I visited a painter of nearly 90 who paints canvases with vibrant reds. And I said to her: 'Your pictures celebrate life.'

She answered close to my ear, a gleam in her eyes: 'I create them for myself, to amuse myself.'

Her wrinkled countenance and body already bent gave off a joy of life that caused me the most admissible of envies. For an instant I desired to have reached, at last, the same landing – where many things for which I now struggle and suffer might be a tranquil celebration.

A woman of 60 took me by the arm, led me to a corner, and whispered, 'Why do they decree that women of our age are finished?' and she had tears in her eyes.

'I don't know,' I said, 'but neither you nor I are finished, I am certain of that. My body has changed but I am still the same.'

My interlocutor was a beautiful woman with grown-up children and close friendships. The gap in her soul was that of self-esteem, because a foolish society would not accord her the right to feel full, and imposed even on her active and capable mind the concept that now she was worth much less than at the age of 40. And each year, each day, she would be worth still less.

'I would give everything, every bit of it, to have my experience of now on the body of when I was 30!' we hear.

'I treat my body well, this great cat,' a poet wrote with the sensibility of artists, and of simple people. 'After all it has served me well so far, and every day I like it more, and the capability it retains.'

Liking the old body with its need for care and love, of more training to function properly, and patience because it is not always what I remember it once was, is a form of happiness that experience can teach.

～

A few decades ago our life expectancies changed, plus our ideas about youth, maturity and old age. We began to live longer. We did not always begin to live better. This seems to me an extraordinary squandering of our era.

My grandmothers, much younger than I am now, seemed to me – and must have felt – old: slow and slightly rheumatic, dark clothes, grey hair, glasses on the tip of the nose, making puddings or knitting. True that my grandmothers were seen subsequently with book in hand – there was much reading in my home. Even so, for us children they were old ladies. Unimaginable that they could have been small girls and young women. 'Grandmother made love some time, at least to have Daddy and Auntie,' was a repulsive notion. Father and mother having a love life in the remote era when they married seemed strange enough to us.

Today's grandmothers drive their car, travel, dine out with friends, date, use the computer and generally speaking seem much happier than the ladies hitherto.

But, ambiguous as we are, there is the contrary factor of an increasingly common rejection of old age.

I remember a television advertisement showing an elderly woman with a shawl on her shoulders and a shrivelled desolate countenance wandering along a corridor. She opened doors and contemplated the empty rooms where her fantasy raised the echo of the voices of children, of her husband. It was the image of the wretched and abandoned old lady who had lost everything – because she had lost her youth.

I do not see why, instead of this grim theatre of old age, one could not transform a child's room into a television parlour, a studio for painting or pottery, a guest room where a woman friend could spend the weekend, or a room for the grandchildren.

If accommodation has no more direct purpose, why should I forfeit my right to it?

Even if my house is not as busy as it was years ago, why should I have to move to a smaller space – unless I really want to, and so decide to as it is more practical, more reasonable? Never due to the belief that I do not need, or, worse, do not deserve it, or that it will no longer be useful.

We are complete human beings at every stage, in the completeness of that stage. It takes effort for us to believe this in old age, just as in adolescence it was difficult to have confidence in ourselves and in our choices for the future.

Our old age comes with a right and a duty to look for new interests and change others, to have joy and pleasures, whatever they might be. I may not in old age be an athlete in bed or even be attracted by a sex life, but I am capable of exercising my joy with friends, my tenderness with the family, my pleasure in walks, in gardening, in reading, in looking at art.

However, in a society in which success and happiness are reduced to money, appearance and sex, if we are mature or old we are discarded. Every day will be a day of disenchantment. Instead of living we shall be consumed. Instead of conquering we shall be, literally, devoured by our phantasms – *to the extent that we permit it.*

This is our potential, our greatness or our defeat: to live with naturalness – or experience like a sudden chastisement from the gods – the new age of 70 or 80 years.

Some people seem to plummet suddenly from careless youth to crabby age. They were caught unprepared. They had never thought about it. They were heedless. A sad way to speed through what is, after all, the miracle of existence.

We imagine we are fooling the machine of time, but its gears trip us instead of driving us. For someone who thinks only of the disenchantments of maturity, *I speak of the enchantment of maturity.* For someone who knows only the resignation of old age, *I remind him of the potential wisdom of old age.*

I need to move ahead with my time. But what is, where is, in what place is *my time*?

Our ears are full of choruses, such as: 'my time has passed', 'I should not', 'where did you ever see' . . . Losing leaves us vulnerable, with fear that this will happen again. That the loved one will forget us, the other die; that charm is extinguished, the party over. We do not want this recurrence, we do not want to lose anything more – we prefer not even to gain something.

But if we listen carefully to our inner voice, there is the persistent reminder of moments of rejoicing and beautiful experiences telling us that life is still possible. It gives some small discreet signals we may be slow to understand.

One of my dearest friends is almost 90 years old, and I look foward each weekend to having a drink with her, in her cosy home, an end-of-Sunday-afternoon whisky. We always have something to talk about. She knows everything, is up-to-date, and takes an interest. She does not choose to talk about her health, which is no longer what it was 10 years ago. She comments on things in the newspaper, politics, music. She asks about friends. She no longer goes to the cinema, but as she is an avid reader, there are a thousand things to talk about.

She likes to laugh and we have a great time.

Thinking of her and others like her, I wonder if to be aged 80 or more will really be a verdict of guilt or if it can be the crowning moment of life. True that to have a 'crowning' there must be a reasonable structure to be 'crowned'. A free-flowing structure of victories and losses, but equally of elaboration and accumulation, lived with enjoyment and grief, with good affections and others less good.

The luminous scale of the positive weighs heaver than that of dismal things.

~

'On youth, what do you say?' I am asked.

I do not need to talk so much about it because it is celebrated and praised in all the communications media, in all the drawing rooms, in all the rooms. It is razzle-dazzle and affliction, growth and ineptitude, anxiety and ecstasy as in all our stages – except that everything there is compressed in intensity and brilliance.

But I do not believe that it is the only one worthwhile, the only one which counts.

Just as I do not argue that maturity and old age are better. They are different, with their good and disastrous sides. Age does not provide the measure of goodness and charm.

The old man always a good guy is a myth, the sweet old lady may be common in story books, but the reality is very different. The old man might actually be a bully, wielding over the family the notorious tyranny of the weakest, the sick, the spoiled child.

Some people, on ageing, become unbearably demanding, querulous, difficult to live with. Fixated on a past with goods, presences, an appearance and activities they can no longer have, they do not adapt.

It is not always the case that the old man is isolated because the children are ingrates. Often it is he who drives them away, with constant criticism of everything and everyone, demands for attention that is not always possible. In the reduced nuclear family of today, in which generally both husband and wife work, the children are few, a maid is very expensive, support for the old man becomes difficult if he is dependent. Good clinics are rare and expensive. A serious problem for everyone. Each family resolves it as it can, generally with financial sacrifice and emotional burden.

'The problem with the old is that there is nothing for them to do, they have no pastimes,' people say, as if it were an inevitability. It is not inevitable. Why should the old man not have *his will* so long as he is independent, so long as his mind is clear – the greatest of benefits as long as it does not mean merely being free of physical pain?

At an advanced age interests need not or cannot be the same as before: activity, money, travel, conquests. At a certain point *the possibilities change but the person is not rendered null and void*. Well-being and joy are found in more trivial things: this is something we learn with time. For this reason, at this point it is simpler to be happy.

New affections are possible at any age: new ties can always be established with people, things, places, interests. Not even love, tenderness and sensuality are the privilege of youth.

But very often the old are not allowed the slightest independence, even if it is perfectly viable.

'What an idea, Mother, to go into the street on your own!'

'Daddy, are you crazy, to live on your own? Travel alone, go to the restaurant alone? At your age . . .'

This is the guilty verdict: at your age, at my age. We do not lose joy, health, love affairs: we rob ourselves of them. And we boycott ourselves by adopting common expressions, such as these:

'I am an old woman, my hands are ugly, I won't wear my rings any more.'

'Why buy a new suit, if I'm old? How many times will I still wear it?'

'Why buy new clothes, why paint the house, why repair the sofa, if I'm old?'

So it is decreed that old men wear trousers too wide, warped shoes, dishevelled hair, and sit on a frayed sofa. It is worth asking what strength they themselves attach to the labels regarding their age, conforming to this cliché at great sacrifice. When they might still have another option.

The time has always to be my time, to achieve something positive and plausible – even if only to change the position of a chair (maybe a wheelchair) for a better view of the falling rain.

An old lady lives alone but enjoys friendships, family, books and music, nature. From time to time she opens a bottle of champagne and makes a toast, on her own (not tearful): to the good things she had, the good things she has, and to one or more she still intends to experience.

One day I showed her my admiration for this.

With a smile, between timidity and amusement, she replied that there was always something to celebrate.

It was a privilege to be alive with an understanding of this, and without serious health problems. She could value the morning light, the aroma of food, the perfume of people. Communicate, know the news, which might range from sport to music, to politics, to . . . whatever she wishes. Still take part.

I was touched by this positive vision of a woman being old. Her age was not a point of stagnation, but of calmly doing things she could not do before. She no longer had to accomplish so many chores nor match so many expectations.

'I think people are more indulgent with me,' she said with a sly smile. 'They must think, "She's a poor old thing"; and so I can finally take a deep breath and be more . . . natural.'

I once read a story more or less thus:

A young woman ran to keep in shape. She passed a little old lady who was cultivating her garden in front of the house, and shouted in passing, *'Granny, if I were as thin as you, I wouldn't need to be running like this!'*

The little old lady signalled her to stop, came up to her and said to her with a smile, 'My girl, when people are as old as I am, everything is easier. People can even retire and enjoy growing roses.'

But if we dream only of a journey to the moon, growing roses might seem too dull, and we shall cultivate nothing.

Our life is always our own, at the age of 12, of 30, of 70. We can make something of it even when we are told no. Within the limits, of the possible, of the sensible (even sometimes of the foolish), we can. We shall only be nothing if we believe we deserve less than everything it is still possible to gain.

Mourning and rebirth

The team of psychologists and psychiatrists who work in a great hospital ask me for a talk on *losses*. The loss of a beloved or the loss of health itself, and the imminence of death.

What could I say to them, competent professionals who on a daily basis were facing the rivers of grief, fear, hope and death that flow in a great hospital? In this all of them, even the young ones, had much more experience than me.

So I tried to keep it simple. To speak of the natural difficulties in dealing with any loss.

First, we do not want to lose.

It is logical not to want to lose. We should not have to lose anything: neither health, nor affection, nor loved ones. But reality is different: we experience a continual seesaw of losses and gains, of which this book seeks to speak.

Second, losing does hurt.

There is no way of avoiding suffering. It is foolish to say 'don't suffer, don't cry'. Grief is important, as is mourning – so long as this does not paralyse us for too much of the time still remaining to us.

Third, we need interior resources to face tragedy and death.

The support of others, the embrace, the listening, the shoulder, even food in the mouth are relative and passing. The decisive strength has to come from us: from where our baggage was stowed. Dealing with the loss will depend on what we shall find there.

Tragedy brings out unsuspected strengths in some people. However devouring it may be, the very suffering that brings us low contributes to return and growth.

For others, everything is destruction. In their interior void roars a gale of revolt and bitterness. The loss strikes them as a personal injustice and a betrayal of life.

Stricken by news of a serious illness, in the knowledge that one may soon die or lose their beloved, people beat their head against a high and unforgiving wall. I am not talking only of the sad rituals of infirmity and death. I am talking of something even more serious: *seeing no more meaning in anything. Because until the day of the loss we were living without thinking.*

We ran bewildered, without reflecting on and perhaps without appreciating what we are now losing, what we enjoyed: a person, health, love, status, everything. If we live superficially, at the moment of reaching into ourselves we find desolation.

I do not believe we should all be philosophers, anchorites or fanatics of any religion. I do not believe in poses and postures. I do not even believe in much theorising over life, death, grief.

But I believe in affection and I am aware that we are part of a mysterious life cycle that endows us with meaning. And though insignificant within the cycle, we are important.

This is one of the reasons why maturity and old age have secrets, beauty and virtues that did not reveal themselves so fully before.

~

In this debate on losses I observe how poorly we deal with one another's grief. We take it as almost a duty to be suddenly full of joy and to seem happy, a matter of hygiene, like taking a bath and being perfumed.

But sometimes we must allow ourselves to suffer – or permit another to suffer.

All of us, friends, families, therapists, doctors, feel strongly our own limitation when someone suffers and we cannot help. At certain moments it is better not to try to interfere, only to offer our presence and respond if we are called. Let the other know we are there.

But not to allow the normal span of grief is unrealistic. At a time of suffering we do not have to ask permission for feeling – and draining – grief.

Suffering, poverty, disease, abandonment, death: these are threats, foreign bodies in a society whose slogans seem to be to act, to bear, to not stop, to not think, to not suffer.

Grief is inconvenient.

Quietude is disturbing.

Retreat intrigues and disturbs the most: 'He must be ill, must be in a bad way, see it's depression, maybe a drink problem, a new lover, a new boyfriend . . .' To avoid anxiety, to avoid 'stopping to think', or merely because they love us and our suffering upsets them, they are constantly giving us a shove: 'React, let's go, leave the house, stop crying, put on a pretty dress, let's go to the cinema, let's go and eat out.'

The right time for this will come too. Mourning is necessary – or the grief will remain buried under futility, its root burying itself even more deeply, its fire burning our last reserves of vitality, and blocking all exits.

I am not going to cheer myself up by dining out when I have lost my love, lost my health, lost my friend, lost my job, lost my illusion – lost something that hurts, whatever it may be.

So, for a moment, a week, a month or more, let me suffer.

Allow me mourning for a sensible period. Help me by not interfering too much. Telephone, give flowers, visit, hug, yes, but please, do not constantly and mercilessly ask me for joy.

If we are not too ill or disturbed, the grief will end of its own accord. If we can hear the call – that may even be a friendly note.

Something positive will make us take the first step out of the emotional intensive care to which the loss has consigned us. One day we peer at the corridor, we go from intensive care to the hospital ward; finally we look into the street and we are in motion again.

We are still alive, still in the process, until death.

~

The loss of love by the end of love, by abandonment or betrayal, overwhelms all our philosophy of life, our values, despite ourselves.

Losses and Gains

Nothing comforts, nothing consoles. As the other is still there, living, perhaps with someone else, our anguish and feeling of rejection are mixed with discord and the potentially harmful attempts to recover someone who no longer wants us.

A woman, rejected by her lover, insisted that he should console her: 'You are the only person I can talk to about us,' she said. Grief made her wound herself even more. She had to endure more time and anguish before finally freeing herself from the man who threw her over, irritated with the impossible demands of the sufferer.

On many occasions, more than we would imagine, a new love is waiting for us. When this does not appear and time is running out, although there will always be a time for loving – even at the age of 80 – we learn other forms of loving. They are not a substitute but they bring light: friends, family, something new, a pastime.

Perhaps losing makes us love better something that will only be taken from us at the final moment: life itself.

Loss of health is compensated for by the palliatives or improvements that medicine brings. Loss of money or employment can be remedied, even though this may demand new boundaries and conditions. Loss of youth is to do with how empty we are or how narrow our horizons.

But the loss of love taken by death is the loss of losses.

It obliges us to go through scenarios of our least known interior: that of our beliefs, our spirituality, in short our transcendence. Learning to lose the loved one is after all learning to gain oneself for oneself, and to gain, in another way – by really taking it on board – all the good that person represented (though in the daily routine people took no notice).

A dear friend went through an experience like that of many devoted women: keeping up with a long illness of someone who was once handsome and attractive and good, the master of himself. But now he was gradually declining, feeling afraid, wanting to live, struggling between impossible optimism and pathetic despondency.

We might weep with him or don the mask of serenity. Talk, be silent, challenge – sometimes flee; every case is absolutely and intimately special.

The final confrontation is not an unexpected fact, much less isolated. It is only the last in a long series of concrete facts and of interior conquests: each of us *makes his own path* – in the literal sense.

We pass through the torture of the pomp and circumstance of funeral and burial (above all of someone on show to the public), and what follows is this strangest, saddest aspect of fatality: *the silence of death.*

No friendly word or gesture can help. One must wait for the effect of time – which is not merely a devourer of days and hours, but also an effective nurse.

'You write obsessively of death, why?' the journalist asks.

No, I do not write obsessively about death, but about life.

In which death plays a part.

It is also incorrect that in my literature I am defeatist or bitter. For anyone who can read it, all that I write is drawn from solidarity with my characters, who are not real people but inventions; from an intense love, and an undeniable hope.

I write about things that exist and are marvellous and others that are frightful, and some that could be better. I write about love and life in all its forms. So I must also necessarily speak of death.

As rather a literary turn, I may say that it is death that writes about us – from our birth it is with us, shaping our route. Death is the great character, the eye that gazes sleeplessly upon us, the voice that summons us and we do not want to heed, but it can show us many secrets.

The greatest of these must be: *death makes life so significant!*

Since we are going to die, we must be able to say today that we love, to do today what we desire so much, embrace today the child or friend. We must be decent today, generous today; we must try to be happy today.

Death does not pursue us: it only awaits us, since we run to its bosom. How we shall reach it is something we can decide in all the years of our time.

Best of all, it reminds us of our transcendence.

We are more than body and anxiety: we are mystery, which makes us greater than we think we are – greater than our own fears.

When love comes close to this area of the unheard, it has to bend: with grief, with terror, it surrenders to this greater proof. It begins to have tenderness; comes close to something called permanence.

If we believe that living is only eating, working, love-making, shopping and paying bills, the death of a loved one will bring unremitting despair. We do not accept, we do not believe in anything more.

But if we have a positive vision of everything including the undesired, unfathomable but inevitable transformation in death, after a while the beloved is adjusted to another strain in us: a continuing part of our reality.

Reality is transfigured, but still exists.

Losing without losing the self

'With the passing of the years it is less painful,' I was told by a friend who 30 years earlier had lost a daughter in childhood.

I know a little of Lady Death. Twice the Beautiful Lady caught me hard, spat in my face, threw me to the ground. Each time it was an important part of me. But I am not like those animals who can remake their lost parts: I do not feel mutilated, although each day I feel inside me those empty spaces that will not come back to be filled.

I learned that the best tribute I can make to the one who has departed is to live as he would like me to live: well, integrally, healthily, with possible joys and impossible plans.

~

Maturity taught me fine and beautiful things (I did not always learn the lesson well). I hope that old age, when it arrives, may teach me even more, and find me more receptive.

I relearned something from childhood that I had forgotten in the rush of family and profession. Like all children – if we do not smother them too much – I liked to be on my own, quiet and totally happy looking at the plates in a book, listening to the wind and the rain or the voices in the house.

As adults we come to fear solitude, perhaps because we regard it as isolation, which can also occur in an inhabited home. We are losing the capacity to be integrated with the universe, even the tiny universe of a patch of garden or a child's nursery. We deprive ourselves of the necessary seclusion that will sometimes refill us with the fuel of reflection, silence and the most natural feeling for things.

In my home today, essential affections populate me. There is no isolation. Friends of all ages also come to see me. Some for trivial and cheerful matters. Others for severe anxieties that I certainly did not know how to handle in my youth. On most of these occasions I do not know what to tell them: no suggestion, no sparkling phrase. But perhaps they sense that by this time I have seen, lived, heard, observed many things.

Little surprises me.

Almost nothing shocks me.

Everything touches me, distresses me and moves me: the most routine, and the most unexpected. Everything shapes a scenario and a path. Maturity makes me love with fewer afflictions and maybe less frivolity – but no less joy.

~

As I am not disabled, I travel alone when necessary. I go into a restaurant alone, I drive my car alone. There are still women who, when we plan a lunch or a dinner, wait for me at the door of the restaurant because they cannot go in without being accompanied. I am not speaking of forsaken housewives without culture, or of peasant women who have never been to a restaurant.

It is not natural for a mature woman to be afraid of going into a restaurant alone. It is not natural to deny oneself living because of someone else's opinion. It is not natural to be ashamed to love, to desire, at any age. It is unnatural to have no more plans at the age of 70.

What is essential is that what I am living should be *my life*: not one that others, society, the media want to impose. It should be unfolding and opening. In this universe of a thousand resources and artifices, fantastic artefacts and innovations, activity and effervescence, I should hold on to my place, where I feel good, where I am at ease – not asleep.

Where I can still believe: makes little difference what, as long as it is not only in evil, violence, betrayal, corruption, negation.

And so that the plot of our story should be one of a royal voyage: not a band of frightened rats running after their own reflections in a hall of mirrors.

5

The time of life

If there is a time to return,
I shall come back.
I shall climb, thrusting the soul
with my blood
through labyrinths and paradoxes
– until it should drown the heart anew.

(Perhaps I shall have the same ardour
as of old.)[1]

The tone of our life

I wanted to write a small practical book on the continual reinvention of ourselves.

In it I said, above all for myself: do not be excessively ineffectual or fearful, because life is to be sipped not like a cup that is emptying, but one that is refreshed at every drop that is drunk.

[1]Lya Luft, *Mulher No Palco*, Sao Paulo: Ediciones Siciliano e Mandarim, 1984

Losses and Gains

As long as there is clear-sightedness it is possible to look around and within us: a pause that may come between the everyday scramble, appointments, shopping, TV, computer, snack bar, drugs, sex without affection, disaffection, spite, wailing, hesitation and resignation.

To reflect is to traverse the superficial.

But if I were crouched in a corner covering my face I should not hear the rush of the wind in the world's trees – which I always wanted so much to comprehend even for one day, perhaps the final day. Nor would I know if the scale of the inevitable losses would outweigh that of the possible gains.

～

We are tenants of something much greater than our own small secret. *It is the powerful cycle of existence.* In that cycle all the calamities and all the beauty have meaning as stages in a process.

We are part of it like the trees in the forest: one tree is struck in its prime and potency, and falls. Another never manages to grow, and perishes; another, very ancient, is bent and twisted, and almost begs for final rest – but can still have dignity and beauty in its condition.

In these pages I spoke of the passage of time that apparently takes everything and returns everything like the tides, but drowns us only to the extent that we allow. I spoke of the time of birth and budding, which is seen as threat and suffering – time that must be tamed to avoid destroying us.

I spoke of losses and gains that depend on the prospect and potential of someone weaving his history.

I declared that it was necessary to find here the tone to allow me to engage in dialogue with the reader, as we all seek the tone according to which we wish – or are able – to exist.

The tone may not even be our own, but a false, mimicked, out-of-tune tone because it is superficial, or tuneful for growing from the soul, the root of our desire, our nature, our entire potential.

Some people may never find it.

Some people cannot follow their rhythm since they do not hear or understand, busily attempting to cover up the obvious. Others discover it and are in step with its movements: quick, calm, passionate, solemn, tragic, slow and quick again. They do not dance with the scarecrow of preconceptions and illusions, but with their lover – *life*.

It is easier to hear the positive tone at 40 than at 20, even easier at 60. I imagine that at 80 we shall have sufficient silence and interior space for it to settle down, settle in and sing.

I return to the start of this book, as I like to do: *The world has no subsistence without our perception that imbues it with form, without our thinking that gives it order.*

∿

To live, as perhaps to die, is to recreate oneself at every moment. Art and artifice, practice and invention in the mirror put before us when we are born. Some visions will be mirages: islands of floating algae that will sink us. Others will hang on branches too high for our timid hope. Yet others shine, but people do not notice them – or do not believe in them.

Life is not there only to be endured or lived, but to be

enhanced. Sooner or later reprogrammed. Conscientiously carried out.

It is unnecessary to achieve anything spectacular.

But the minimum must be the maximum that we can make of ourselves.

~

I end the book and I switch off the computer knowing that however writers write, the musicians compose and sing, the painters and sculptors play with shapes, colours and lighting – however the parallel context of art expresses the profound contradiction of human sentiment, dances before us and summons us to the last thread of clear-sightedness, the essence has no name or shape: it is discovery and dread, glory or damnation of each of us.